D1491671

THE SCOTTISH RUGBY BOOK '94

THE
SCOTTISH
RUGBY
BOOK '94

EDITED BY

IAN McLAUCHLAN

**SCOTTISH
RUGBY UNION**

MAINSTREAM
PUBLISHING

EDINBURGH AND LONDON

in association with

The Royal Bank of Scotland

First published in Great Britain in 1993 by
MAINSTREAM PUBLISHING COMPANY (EDINBURGH) LTD
7 Albany Street
Edinburgh EH1 3UG

ISBN 1 85158 578 8

A catalogue record for this book is available from the British
Library

Phototypeset in Palatino by Intype, London

Printed in Great Britain by Butler and Tanner Ltd, Frome

Contents

**The Royal Bank
of Scotland**

Foreword

SPORTING ACHIEVEMENT DESERVES
THE BEST IN WORDS AND IMAGES

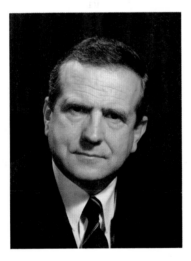

Customers and tourists visiting our traditional home and flag-ship branch at 36 St Andrew Square often register a double-take before they enter Britain's loveliest banking hall. What have the two splendid paintings which celebrate Scotland's finest rugby moments of recent years got to do with banking?

The two paintings, *The Turning Point 1984* and *Underdog Rampant 1990*, were commissioned by the Royal Bank to honour the achievement of Scotland's rugby players in two of the most dramatic of the 33 Royal Bank internationals to be staged at Murrayfield. On both those occasions, Scotland triumphed in the final game of the season in a head-to-head battle for the

Grand Slam, firstly against the Auld Ally and finally against the Auld Enemy. It is not often that a sponsor manages to combine arts and sports sponsorship in a single venture. We were naturally delighted that prints of the 1990 painting sold in record numbers.

It is in the same spirit – the belief that sporting achievement deserves the very best of recognition in words and images, in a more lasting form than even our best newspapers can provide – that we continue our support of this venture by our good friends at the Scottish Rugby Union. Last year's publication set standards which this *Scottish Rugby Book* handsomely matches.

We are proud to be associated with the publication and I am sure that all those people who make up the band of Scottish rugby supporters, whether they display their enthusiasm on the pitch, along the touchline or in front of the television, will welcome this new addition to their bookshelves.

Dr George Mathewson
Chief Executive
The Royal Bank of Scotland

Introduction

Ian McLauchlan

It was a year of rugby at the top level when so near became so far. Scotland came close in Paris but failed to take their chances and the challenge faded once again. The repeat of an old story. At Twickenham, the departure of Craig Chalmers heralded the complete breakdown of the back line in defence and attack. Was one player ever so sorely missed since the squad system was introduced? Two handsome home wins against Ireland and Wales salvaged the season. The first, against Ireland, was achieved in appalling conditions which inhibited the home side much more than their visitors. Victory against Wales showed Scotland at their best.

The disappointment of only five Scots in the Lions party and the absence of Andy Nicol and Doddie Weir in particular was partially offset by the appointment of Gavin Hastings as captain. Rumblings were heard that he did not have the complete support of the management team but he rose above that to become a modern-day colossus both on and off the field. The Lions themselves were a disappointment and the lack of Scots in the Test teams for the second and third games against New Zealand was difficult to comprehend at home. Scotland's poor showing in the inaugural World Cup Sevens tournament was offset by a highly successful tour by the Development Squad to the South Sea

Bob McInnes (Deputy Managing Director, Branch Banking Division) and Gregor Townsend with The Royal Bank of Scotland Young Player of the Year award

Islands. The squad lost only one game, the last, to Western Samoa who then went on to a highly successful tour of New Zealand.

1993 saw the opening of the new North and South Stands at Murrayfield and the demolition of the West Stand. The 1994 season will see the new Murrayfield open as one of the finest stadiums in the world. A new development in Scottish rugby took place at Murrayfield on Friday, 23 April 1993 with the first ever *Herald* Scottish Rugby Awards Dinner. A full house saw Gregor Townsend (Gala) become The Royal Bank of Scotland Most Promising Young Player of the Year. Melrose were clear winners of the McEwan's Team of the Year, while Gary Armstrong, the Jed-Forest and Scotland scrum-half, was proclaimed winner of *The Herald* Player of the Year award. Each prize-winner received a cheque for £1,000 plus a very handsome trophy from each of the sponsors. The awards dinner was highly successful and will become one of the highlights of the rugby season from now on.

The Royal Bank
of Scotland

Poacher Turned Gamekeeper

THE SCOTTISH RUGBY UNION'S
NEW MEDIA ADVISER
ON HIS FIRST SEASON

Brian Meek

They say your sins will find you out; in a journalist's case it is usually his or her words. A couple of years ago, for a book entitled *Feet, Scotland, Feet* (published by who else but Mainstream?), I wrote a chapter detailing some of my own experiences in covering the game we all love. I also had a couple of mild swipes at the Scottish Rugby Union. 'The SRU,' I told the readers, 'should have appointed a press relations officer years ago. It is simply not adequate to expect secretary Bill Hogg to field queries about everything from the selection of the international team to how many pies are on sale at Murrayfield.'

Shortly after that book was published I was in Ireland with the Scotland party for the opening Five Nations Championship match at Landsdowne Road. On the eve of the game I came back after dinner to the Westbury Hotel and bumped into Bob Munro, the former chairman of the selectors and general committee man . . . and an old friend. As my memory has it, we did not actually sit down, nor even have a drink, but prowled up and down the lobby like two advocates discussing a case. Which was not too far from the truth.

I had heard the Union was looking for someone to give advice on the media and public relations and was intrigued to know to whom they might turn. Perhaps Bob was about to tell me. 'The committee were wondering whether you would be prepared to help?' he said. That statement stirred in me very mixed emotions. My relationships with the SRU had often followed a rocky road: over 20 years ago they had, after all, banned me from playing for simply doing my job. I had had various brushes with selectors and one of their number had threatened violence when he did not like something I had written. For years I had been a consistent critic of what I saw as the Union's intransigence over rewards to players at the top level, their refusal to announce sentences for sending-off, their attitude towards individual awards. Now I was being asked to play in a quite different position.

Yet if you spend a great deal of time criticising there comes a point, and this has happened to me before, when someone says: 'OK, if you are so smart, why not tell us your ideas?' I felt the challenge was being made. Could I, after all I had said, simply opt out? 'We don't have to decide anything tonight,' soothed Mr Munro, as cunning as the guy Red Riding Hood bumped into, 'just put your thoughts on paper and we can discuss it further.' I did, and was asked to attend a committee meeting in the Carlton Hotel.

Has any outsider, any press man, ever addressed the SRU committee, I wondered, as I sat waiting to go in, feeling for all the world like a soldier about to face his court-martial. Coach Ian McGeechan was on before me and emerged smiling: 'They are in a good mood, you'll be all right.' I bet he says that to everybody. Gordon Masson, the then president, welcomed me and, to put me at ease, offered a cigarette. That was kind, but unfortunately I had just given up smoking, and so was even more nervous! Anyway I launched into what was probably a tendentious spiel, saying what I thought should happen. My theme, I suppose, was that the SRU had to do more to put their ideas across, be prepared to argue their point, give out more information, brush up their image, act like the major organisation they are.

There was one question, from Ian Laughland of London Scottish. 'You are going to go on writing for your newspaper. What happens if we decide something and you want to attack us in print?' I replied along these lines. 'That could happen. I cannot promise to support everything that the committee decides and, anyway, that is not the role which his being suggested. I will give the advice, it is up to you whether it is accepted or not.'

They thanked me and I left, heading for the nearest bar. Bill Hogg told me later I was now the Union's media and public relations adviser, the first ever. My colleague Bill McMurtrie said the appointment was the 'poacher turned gamekeeper' which was fair comment. I had accepted the post, however, because I believed it could be of benefit to both the hunter and the hunted.

So how has the first year been? Fascinating. Right from the start I was given access to all the relevant information; no one tried to be obstructive. I was lucky to have Robin Charters as president, a man already widely liked and respected by the media, a hard guy to dislike. Early on, the BBC – not the sports department – decided to set up a radio programme in which the Union would play the role of bad guys and would be fired at from all sides. Robin went on, smiled, accepted some of the points made, faced down the critics and walked off, having taken game, set and match. International weekends make special demands on presidents who often have to entertain royalty, heads of state, leading politicians, sponsors and visiting committee men. In addition, they are expected to encourage the team and make several speeches. I never wrote a speech for Robin but we would chat about the theme before he spoke and he would then deliver the oration in his inimitable and amusing style. There was nothing stuffy about President Charters.

I thought it was part of my job to make sure that the facilities offered to my media colleagues were improved. This was particularly difficult in the past year because of the rebuilding of part of the stadium. Still, I hope they felt they had proper access to players immediately after the internationals and noticed a small improvement in the catering. When the new Main Stand is completed I think we will have press facilities as good as anything else being offered.

One of my first tasks was to establish an SRU magazine, *The Voice*. This is circulated to all clubs and is an opportunity to highlight, in greater depth than newspaper coverage will allow, issues in the game. Ian McGeechan has written for this publication, as have Douglas Morgan and Allan Hosie plus my regular correspondent Iain Goodall whom I am determined to shape into a journalist (well, he wasn't much of a referee). I should like to get a lively letters column started in the magazine, one of my tasks for this season. For I am well aware that the Union must develop better relationships with its own member clubs. That means a continuing dialogue on the issues, everything from the league structure to the payment of players. Yes, Murrayfield has been remote at times but there has also been a tendency to lay at the door of the SRU problems that the clubs themselves will not face up to... like field discipline, for instance.

My first year in post has not been without troubles. A group of local residents did attempt to hold up the whole redevelopment scheme: winning that one was just as important as success in any international. There were lively debates about the introduction of the Irish Provincial matches. The selection of the Lions party was anything but uncontroversial. There were lots of complaints about no tickets being on sale on the first day of the World Cup Sevens, a matter over which the Union had absolutely no control but were still blamed.

This season the Union plans to hold meetings throughout the country, giving the opportunity for club committee men and players to put over their views. Only by listening to one another can we all learn. My appointment was a small matter yet it represents another change in Union attitude. Sometimes I wonder if we all realise how far we have come in the last decade.

We have now, in Murrayfield, one of the finest sporting stadiums in all of Europe. Our friends in soccer are frankly envious and I predict they will ask to use our facilities on an occasional basis in the future. In the last ten years Scotland have won two Grand Slams and finished fourth in the World Cup. Our leading coaches, not to forget our top referees, are widely respected throughout the world. The SRU structure itself has been considerably revamped. As well as a chief executive there is now a director of rugby – and a fine one at that – and a proper coaching set-up. Remember all those articles we wrote demanding a more professional approach? The concept of the team manager is accepted, not just for the national XV, but also for the A side and the Under-21s. Selectors are becoming fewer but more powerful. I can recall arguing for that a long time ago. Is it not significant, too, that over a recessionary period, sponsors have been ready to put up substantial sums of money to be involved in our game? They are not charitable organisations; they are investing in rugby because they believe there is a good return.

Of course, everything in the garden is not rosy. I think we need another look at the structure, that there is room for a national cup, and that we must face up to the problem of too many games burning out too many players. It is just that I get tired of the moaning minnies telling us everything is wrong all the time. Yes I have a vested interest, but for a nation of our size, I think we are rather good at running and playing rugby. But don't let us just listen to an old fogey, let us hear from a coach and from a player:

I went to see Richie Dixon for a number of reasons. In the late seventies the former Jordanhill flanker had proved to be an inspiring captain of the Scotland B team, indeed many of us felt he was extremely unlucky not to win a full cap. From there he graduated, almost naturally one felt, to the role of coach and has been at the heart of that department ever since. Who better to talk to than a man who has been on five overseas tours and is Douglas Morgan's assistant with the national squad? His good lady gave us coffee and we chinwagged for hours. Richie made it clear from the start that the man who had influenced him most was Jim Telfer. 'I think he is the father of the modern Scottish game. In the seventies, after vast experience as a player and being much impressed by the New Zealand ways, Jim virtually decided single-handedly that our style had to change.

15

He wanted us to be ruckers with both hands and feet. At coaching courses, at squad sessions, at dinner he preached the same message with all the zeal of a missionary. He grasped the nettle; we benefited as a result.'

Telfer was expected by many to succeed Bill Dickinson as coach to the international side. Instead the selection committee went for Nairn MacEwan, a more recent player. In retrospect that does still seem an extraordinary decision, one which astonished the aforementioned Dickinson. But perhaps it worked to Telfer's advantage. He turned the B side from France's whipping boys into a formidable, and successful unit. The players, many of them on the way up, would have walked through walls for him. When Nairn MacEwan was forced out by ill-health there was no other credible candidate.

Dixon says: 'The style Jim was after was not a direct copy of the All Blacks, it was actually the manner in which the best of the Border teams had played. He recognised that we do not produce too many heavyweights and went for angular, athletic players.

'People said we kicked and chased a lot. Yes, we did. In the modern game marking is very tight; you have to try to turn opponents in order to breach the gain line. But to suggest that the skill factor was reduced is nonsense. Look at some of the players in Telfer's Grand Slam side of 84: John Rutherford, Roy Laidlaw, David Johnston, David Leslie, Jim Calder and Iain Paxton to name but a few, and watch some of the tries they scored.

'Jim Telfer put the self-belief into Scottish rugby. He organised the defence properly and convinced the players, if they did what he told them, they would reach new heights. They sure did.' Telfer himself said after the campaign: 'The Grand Slam is the start, not the finish.' Yet for a while it did not look that way.

Jim himself took a well-earned rest and was succeeded by his namesake Colin Telfer, one of the most accomplished fly-halves of the post-war era. He had assisted Jim in 84 and was a popular choice among the players. Derrick Grant, hugely successful at Hawick, also became involved at national level. Colin Telfer was downright unlucky. No one was going to find it easy after a Grand Slam; some of the players he inherited,

Richie Dixon

Ian McGeechan

Jim Aitken, Calder, Bill Cuthbertson, Alan Tomes, were coming to the end of their careers. In his first international in charge, against Romania in a baking Bucharest, a dubious refereeing decision swung the game the home side's way. In 1985 every game in the Five Nations Championship was close. Scotland lost them all – to England 10–7, to Wales 25–21, to Ireland 18–15 and to France 11–3. Colin Telfer decided he had had enough.

His friend Derrick Grant soldiered on. 'He was the man who cemented much of the work done by Jim Telfer,' Dixon, already climbing the coaching ladder himself, declares. It was not, however, all down to the coaches; there were active minds being used on Scotland's behalf off the field too. Richie Dixon speaks most highly of successive selectors' chairmen Ian McGregor and Robin Charters. They were both shrewd and receptive; they talked to the coaches and accepted advice; they put the structure in place.

By the time of the first World Cup in 1987 Grant had been joined by another former international and British Lion, Ian McGeechan. Here was another man who would leave giant footsteps across the pages of Scottish rugby history. Dixon holds the man with whom he worked over many years in high regard. 'He is above all a superb communicator. No one could question Ian's commitment, the travelling alone would have sickened many people. Right from the start you could sense his single-mindedness, his attention to detail, his skill at video analysis. His game plans were specific and everybody knew what their role was to be. Of course he was fortunate to have such a good group of players. But, just like Jim Telfer, he made these players better than they ever believed they could be and it is no accident that they came to revere him.'

McGeechan's proudest moments came during the 1990 Grand Slam with a finish no Scot will ever forget. There was also sweet success with the Lions in Australia and disappointment in the most recent British Isles tour to New Zealand. Now McGeechan has gone, for a while anyway, and Morgan has taken over. In which direction are Scotland headed during the next decade? Dixon feels optimistic.

'We had a hard tour to Australia in 1992 but were far from disgraced. A young squad have just distinguished themselves in the South Seas. Our schoolboys completed a successful trip to Oz – I don't think we should be despondent. What we will have to do is what Scotland have always been obliged to do – to make the best of scant resources. If the next ten years are as good as the last there will be few complaints.'

A very young, fresh-faced lad can be spotted in some of the pictures from the 1984 Grand Slam. Douglas Wyllie of Stewart's/Melville sat on the bench all through the Five Nations Championship ... and did exactly the same in 1990. It seems sometimes that Wyllie has always been with us. In fact the polished fly-half-cum-centre is still only 30 years of age. He won his first cap against Australia in 84 and has added 12 more since; however, his real contribution to the Scottish scene has to be as a tourist. No one, with the exception of Peter Dods, has travelled so far in his country's colours.

Wyllie's international touring began in Romania in 84, Jim Renwick's farewell to the scene and Sean McGaughey's one and only cap. The experience in that unfortunate country might have been enough to turn anyone into a home bird but Dougie's passport has rarely been idle. He has been on trips to Canada and America, France, New Zealand (for the first World Cup), Zimbabwe, Japan, New Zealand again, Canada, and the States again and more recently Fiji, Tonga and Western Samoa. Oh, and he was in the Scotland squad for the second World Cup too. John Rutherford and Craig Chalmers have been first-choice fly-halves for most of the last ten years; Wyllie has been the back-up. 'Actually playing alongside Rudd, me in the centre, was one of my more memorable international moments.' He seemed the ideal player to talk about the decade; he grew up during it, after all, and is still going strong, captain of his club and very much involved at district level.

Douglas, a late entrant to rugby – he was soccer-mad until his early teens – shot into the Stewart's/Melville FP first XV after only a handful of games in the minor sides. There was a certain D. W. Morgan at scrum-half for the club then and Wyllie admits to being the willing and eager apprentice. Winning the Middlesex Sevens early on whetted the appetite. At 21 he was in the Scotland squad.

What are the major changes he has witnessed? 'The game

at the highest level is taken more seriously now. It is more concentrated, the profile is greater. When I started, it seemed even Scotland players could have normal jobs and lead ordinary lives. I am not sure that is true anymore. At the very top you just about have to be a full-time player today or at least have a very understanding employer.' He speaks with feeling and experience, having lost a job in the past because of his commitment to rugby. Now he is an agent for Schweppes, one of Scottish rugby's first major sponsors. 'I think we still have to make up our minds what kind of game we want in Scotland. There is not enough money to pay everyone a wage, I realise that, but those giving service at international level will have to be rewarded better.' But are we not constantly told that players do not want to be paid? Douglas Wyllie laughed: 'I don't know who these players are.'

Looking at changes in style, Douglas at first gave the answer that the game was not physically harder than it was when he started. On reflection he amended his comments. 'I recall Keith Robertson and myself, neither of us weighing much soaking wet, playing together in the midfield in my early days. You would be unlikely to find such a combination in an international side now; there is usually at least one basher in the centre and even the wingers are bigger. The changes in the laws mean you have to get the ball back quicker.' But have they produced more skilful players? 'I don't know – there has not been another Renwick, has there?'

Wyllie believes that standards have improved generally although perhaps some of the flair has been lost. He is also one who would increase the influence of district competitions. 'If I could be granted two wishes they would be that I was 18 again and playing for Edinburgh every week against sides like Bath, Bristol, Harlequins, etc. Maybe that is a pipe-dream but if we want to maintain our position in world rugby the top players need to be tested against class opposition more often. Scotland has done superbly well to be in the top half-dozen, considering our resources. We will have to work very hard to stay there.'

Wyllie will be part of that effort. He is loath to hang up the boots – 'you are an awfully long time retired' – but when he does you can bet he will be involved as a coach. Already he

Think tank. Douglas Morgan and Ian McGeechan

sees his mission as bringing on young players in his club and district. That is a refreshing thought, for too many of our top players slip away for good after their last cap. We need not only more properly trained coaches but could do with a number of younger referees as well.

Yet Scotland is extremely lucky in the talent it has in the rugby fraternity. It never ceases to impress me the number of people who are prepared to give so much of their time, with absolutely no material reward, to make it all happen. The guy

Training break

who goes with the third XV and is pressed into running the line, if not refereeing the match; the ladies who, week in, week out, provide the teas, the man who sweeps out the dressing-room, the harassed secretary who hunts to fill the gaps in his teams, the club treasurer, these are the folk who make Scottish rugby what it is.

Yes, there most certainly is a major problem to be faced about whether international players should be paid, and for what (although the sponsorship deal with the Famous Grouse is a step in the right direction); some countries are cheating and ignoring IB regulations with impunity. But let us keep this matter in some kind of proportion. Whatever is decided, the vast majority of rugby players will never earn a penny from the game. What they will receive is years of enjoyment . . . and that is surely a lot more important.

I know what I would do about the payment issue. This is my opinion, not anyone else's and certainly not the SRU's. I would introduce a trust fund to cover all players in the international squad. A sum would be paid into the trust of each member, say £1,000, per season. An extra £500 would be paid for appearing in each international. The players would not be allowed, except in exceptional circumstances, to touch any of the money until they retired. All other cash coming into the game, from whatever source, would be used for development of facilities, an increase in professional staff available to districts, in particular coaches, and at youth and schools level. The trust system may offend the purists but it has the advantage that everyone in the side receives the same return, it gives players an investment for the future, and it makes everything above board. Is that not preferable to the present uncertainties?

Last December I went to see Musselburgh, then challenging for the Second Division Championship. In the Stoneyhill clubhouse there were scores of local pensioners enjoying a Christmas lunch at the expense of the club. Rugby is not just about playing the game, it is also about playing a part in the community. As long as it continues to do that, the future will be bright.

**The Royal Bank
of Scotland**

The Home Front

THE 1992–93 McEWAN'S LEAGUE AND INTER-DISTRICT SEASON

John Beattie

Contemplating writing an article about the McEwan's League and Inter-District season just gone by is a bit like looking forward to a night with Zsa Zsa Gabor – you think 'Oh my god, no!'. Sorry to spoil an old joke, but last season could be summed up simply by saying that Melrose won again, Currie were the surprise package, and two very well-equipped teams in GHK and Dundee HSFP inexplicably dropped out of the frame. But to be that negative would be counter-productive when so much effort was expended by so many in the search for two points. All that effort attracts the media too you know. You would be amazed at the number of rugby players now handing out gems like 'One game at a time' and 'We tried to pressurise the opposition' or, my favourites, 'The tries were just the icing on the cake' and 'Two metres is just my distance'.

So what did happen last year then? Well – lots, I think. The

rules changed for starters amid howls of protest at the unjust-
ness of the team carrying the ball forward into the ruck not
getting the resultant scrum when things ground to a halt and
the ball stayed put. Early season and many of our finest club
sides were experimenting with the rolling maul to try to keep
the ball in hand and away from the opposition. Trying to
change the techniques perfected over a decade's rucking prac-
tices proved a mite harder than expected, and it was a lot
easier for defences to spoil the advance of forwards looking like
lumbering Englishmen from the early eighties, than for attackers
to stop defences from grabbing hold of the ball and ball carrier
with the obvious effect on which side got the put-in.

Isn't it strange how it's so much easier to think of a spoiling
tactic than a creative one. Then, like the light brigade, in came
Melrose to save the day. 'To heck with this chaps', you could
hear them cry in their Border accents 'it's back to rucking and
straightforward driving for us. Oh, and if anyone gets in the
way, we'll tramp them out of the way which means they won't
try to prevent the release of the ball on our side again.' Being
there watching Melrose when they had decided to get back to
basics was a memorable day for me. Someone must have sat
down and thought long and hard, and the right answer came
up.

A by-product of all this law-changing was this fancy
straight maul, with the ball hidden right at the back and the
blockers driving in front of it. It works a peach, especially as
you're not supposed to drop the maul when it's on the go, but
I'm scunnered as to why so few teams try to blitz the thing
while it's in the process of being set up. No one will spot you
pulling it down before it starts trundling irrevocably onwards.

After early season experiments, most of the teams in this
country reverted to rucking, with the added proviso that the
ball carrier was to seek the ground at the earliest opportunity
for safety, and remain in full view of the referee at all times. It
was even obvious at national squad sessions – and so far I've
been pretty good at sneaking in unnoticed into Murrayfield
during closed-door sessions – that all 15 players are now encouraged to run at the opposition, and get to the deck for quick
release. For sure, we're such a small country that we do really

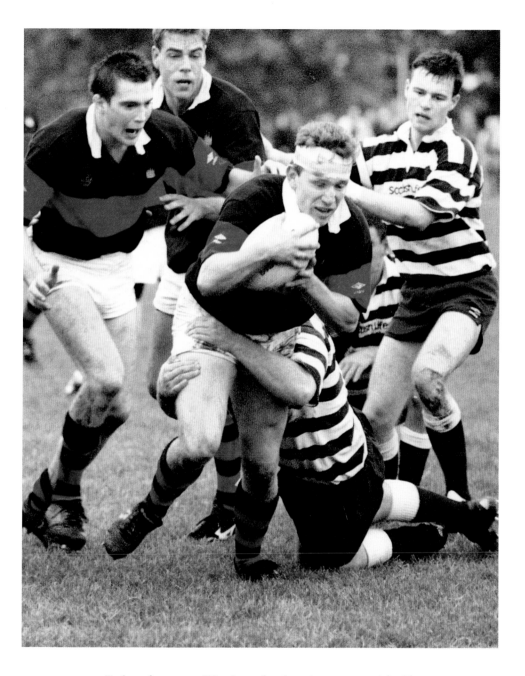

*Badge of courage. Wearing a bandage to cover a cut beside
his right eye, Dundee's Andy Nicol forces his way over for a try despite
being tackled*

all end up doing practically the same thing. Good in some ways, but bad in others maybe.

Then, and it's stressing the point, some of the clubs were revolting. Perhaps it wasn't as big a backlash as was made out at the time, in that all the clubs did was meet to air their opinions, but the astonishing part of it all was the fact that the majority of the senior clubs in Scotland felt that they had to meet at all outwith the annual general meeting of the SRU. It was, of course, all about the clubs apparently not having been consulted about this coming season's increased emphasis on the Inter-District Championship.

Games against Irish provinces now beckon for our better players, and it's open to question as to whether some decide to pick and choose their games. If they do, then the first games they'll avoid are club games. You get selected, they say, from games that bit higher up the ladder – that's why they're there after all. The position is still unresolved, but when the argument was put forward that our better players needed more concentrated rugby, it is doubtful whether games against the Irish were high on the agenda. I think folk thought that Bristol, Bath, Leicester and the like were more inviting. Again though, we're a small enough country to keep talking about it and get there in the end.

Was the rugby good last year then? Well, yes and no. Gary Callander, ex-Kelso and Scotland captain, used to say that rugby players train at least twice a week, for two hours a shot, then play on a Saturday, for about 30-odd weeks. It adds up to hundreds of hours a year practising for the game of rugby. And yet there are inevitably people that arrive at the end of a season still lacking in some of the skills of the game. If you are a coaching fanatic, then the way that teams were schooled last year would have brought a tear of happiness to your eye. If you prefer a spectacle, man beating man, then some of the stuff on offer would only have disappointed. Dundee HSFP, who of course went down, played the most attractive game, but that's not winning rugby. Heriot's started off playing open stuff, which got them into trouble, then battened down the hatches to get themselves out of danger, but perhaps it was Currie, ironically from nearby Balerno, who demonstrated that where there's a will there's a way. Of all the teams in the League, Currie's game was based on support play in the open field, and a dynamic ability and desire to attack the opposition with the ball in hand. Moreover, Currie are one of few teams to stick rigidly to a no-train-no-play regime, which works. And Currie trained four times a week toward the latter part of the season when things really mattered. That was something that all the successful teams of the season managed to force themselves to do, in Currie's case because the players asked for it.

Seasons, though, are best remembered by isolated occurrences that somehow stick in the mind. One day, I drove all the way down to Hawick to cover a match, and when I got there the thing had been called off. Undeterred, I bolted back up the road to watch the last 20 minutes of a Glasgow Accies game – which was a huge mistake. You somehow get used to seeing 16 players arrive at the ball within a count of two or three when you watch the top league, whereas in the Second Division it takes a good deal longer, fewer people turn up to watch, and the skill level isn't as high. Second Division clubs could do well to take a Saturday off and watch, say, a Melrose versus Jed-Forest game to see the commitment. It's easy to get blasé about our rugby up here, but it's good. We just don't have the size.

Then Bill Johnstone and I were doing the commentary on the France-Scotland game in Paris, in what was a pretty good season for the national team. The side still has limited ability I think, but that's irrelevant. Anyway, it was obvious that there had been a cock-up at the French end in booking the lines back to Britain, so the upshot was that no one was going to hear Bill and me. Bill prepares meticulously for the commentaries, and, like me, would actually do them for free if he could, so an air of devastation accompanied the two of us as we sat encased in our glass lookout, high above the ground. It was me, Bill, and no one else. Bill turned to me. 'Johnnie,' he said, 'I've spent so much time preparing for this.' I wondered quietly what was coming next. 'I've decided,' he said, 'I'm going to commentate anyway.' I looked on in disbelief as Bill started. 'It's Gavin Hastings – to his brother Scott – Scott Hasting kicks to touch – and so it's a line-out for the French just outside the Scottish 22 – and I'm pleased to say to all of our listeners that I have beside

Kelso captain John Jeffrey goes to war on GHK

Champagne celebrations for Melrose

me John Beattie – John – give us your impression of the game so far.' I was stunned. It was make or break time. There was nowhere to go. I couldn't let him down. Believe it or not we commentated on the whole damn game – and no one heard a word.

One more little point. This year's League Championship was devalued slightly by the nevertheless important preparations for the World Cup Sevens. Inevitably, had Scotland done better in that event then the withdrawal of players from the Championship would have been so much easier to bear.

But back to facts and figures. Two clubs, Stewartry and Duns, won all of their 13 games in the season, with Duns, going up from the Sixth Division, scoring a massive 585 points along the way, the highest of any club in the League. Allan Glen's, promoted from the Seventh Division had the best defensive record with only 92 points getting past them, while St Boswells, dropping off the bottom of the Third Division, conceded the most points – 480 – followed closely by Strathmore on 414.

At the top of the First Division Melrose had made sure of retaining their title with a 16–7 win against Currie, the 'galloping giraffe' Doddie Weir scoring Melrose's only try of the game, when their nearest rivals, Gala, were beaten by bottom club Dundee HSFP, thereby depriving spectators of a Border play-off that had been eagerly awaited.

At the bottom of the First Division, it was nail-biting stuff right down to the final games. GHK, with all to play for and to be relegated if they lost, fell victim to Currie, who looked to be quite happy where they were in the middle of the table, which says a lot for Currie's pride. Similarly, getting up from the second had drama as part of the occasion, as always. Musselburgh travelled to Stewart's/Melville having led the division all season with the scent of promotion in their nostrils and found themselves 10–0 down at half-time. The visitors fought back to lead 14–10 in front of the 5,000-strong crowd, only to see Dougie Wyllie, the home team's captain, sneak in for a try that was converted by full-back Murray Thomson. Musselburgh

Previous page: *Ian Burnside of Stewart's Melville and Colin Power of Musselburgh battle for possession at the line-out*

had lost 17–14, and at the same time West of Scotland made certain of their own promotion by dumping Grangemouth 52–6 to top Stewart's/Melville on points difference. West of Scotland were champions, Stewart's/Melville drank their champagne anyway as they were going up, while the Musselburgh team looked silent, and lost, in their despair.

It was, of course, the first season with the value of a try increased to five points, and some of the top players took advantage. Gordon MacKay, the big Glasgow Academical loose-forward, helped himself to 13 tries, and that other Second Division player, John McKenzie from Stewart's/Melville, managed nine. Still in the Second Division, Dave Barrett from West of Scotland was the country's top points scorer, notching 202. If we're talking points, then spare a thought for poor Strathmore in the Seventh Division, beaten 127–3 by Ross High who achieved a frightening 21 tries and 11 conversions. An average of a try every four minutes no less, without taking into account the time taken for kicks at goal. That massive score was enough to give the Ross High players promotion as they leap-frogged Holy Cross. Holy Cross had been leading the division by one point, but that barrage of tries from Ross High meant that they missed out on promotion altogether with their own game ending up an 8–8 draw. Tragic really. No wonder grown men cry sometimes.

Now, if you've just dusted this book off the shelf in the twenty-first century, we are still in an era that sees the League straddling the season at both ends, with the District Championship occupying the section after the first half of the League is finished, finishing before the start of the big stuff – the Five Nations. The District Championship is, as mentioned earlier, still the place to do the business if you are a player with aspirations towards higher things because it brings the better players together on the field of combat. Strangely though, it has yet to catch the imagination in the way that top League games do, or the end-of-season sevens. There was no doubting the level of ability of the players in this competition, and McEwan's Inter-District games in season 92–93 were almost always torrid affairs with national team selectors present aplenty, and club companions pitched opposite each other as they sided with their chosen district.

North and Midlands v Glasgow

Glasgow face the South

Champion feeling.
Craig Chalmers

District matches are but mini trials. The South, with an experienced core of international players like Craig Chalmers, Gary Armstrong, Tony Stanger and Derek Turnbull at their disposal, proved too strong for all but Glasgow. Glasgow recorded their only win of the series beating the South 9–7 at Hughenden, while the Scottish Exiles managed to beat only one side – Glasgow – 17–7 at Richmond. Despite the results on paper, five of the Exile pack were placed in the starting line-up for the first international against Ireland. In a series that saw only one draw, a 13–13 scrap between Edinburgh and Glasgow at Goldenacre, the South ran out champions. It must be good fun playing for the South and Melrose.

So the season passed at its usual frantic pace. Craig Chalmers was always there to give a demonstration of the art of winning rugby, Jim Telfer, our best ever coach, stood right behind the posts bawling at his players as always, Melrose and Heriot's proceeded to play a game on ice when the groundsman's pitchfork had bounced off the surface of the pitch when he had tried to fork it. Torville and Dean would have struggled.

Stirling County slipped from their former excellence, but not down a league, and players like John Jeffrey, Gregor Townsend and Andy Nicol were still around to delight. Gary Armstrong just frightened you with his commitment in the royal blue of Jed-Forest.

You can always knock a thing if you want to, but the great thing about rugby, especially ours, is that you can never say it's boring. Bring on next year's McEwan's League and Inter-District Championship.

**The Royal Bank
of Scotland**

The A Team

SCOTLAND'S 1992–93 A-TEAM
GAMES

John Beattie

The A team was something put forward by Ian McGeechan, Scotland's international coach, some years back. The need for the A team arose partly from the fact that in the traditional B fixtures, only Scotland, it appeared, adhered to the policy that players who had already received full caps could no longer represent their country at a level other than full international. Hence the development squad approach to the preparation of better players. Its critics would say that it has its drawbacks. Namely that if full internationalists do play in these matches, and the matches take the place of B games, then they immediately deny other uncapped players the chance to play at that level. Also, they would say, we know what these players can do anyway. Conversely, what better way to prepare a player for a cap than to make him share a room with, or play alongside, someone who has been there and can pass on the knowledge.

Duncan Paterson, Scottish team Manager

Safe in the knowledge that another big year lay ahead in the development of Scottish rugby, the A XV took on four fixtures in the 1992–93 season. Coming on the back of the summer tour to Australia, as this season did, it was no surprise that many internationalists got the chance to shine again down the ladder. For instance, included in the team that took the field against Italy in December were ten full caps, including Gavin and Scott Hastings, Craig Chalmers and Gary Armstrong. They were all British Lions.

The first game though was against Spain in Madrid in September. Team manager Duncan Paterson singled out both Alan Watt, who later went on to win his second cap against Ireland, and Kelso's Adam Roxburgh for high praise. Watt had a hand in two of Scotland's second-half tries, one of which was scored by Roxburgh, just as the national selectors were looking for new faces to fill the back-row berths. Ian Jardine, the Stirling County centre, was another player to impress with his powerful running and tackling in the middle of the field. For this match

Paul Burnell was switched to the loose-head to accommodate Alan Watt on the tight-head, with Doddie Weir and Chris Gray filling the second-row berths. Strange then that Paul Burnell played at tight-head in the Five Nations, Alan Watt at loose-head, and Doddie Weir in the number 8 position. Just shows how people change their minds.

The side rattled in 35 points against the Spanish, but Spain have ambitions to be a 'real' rugby nation, and proceeded to score two tries themselves, one from the excellent Jaime Gutierres.

Mid-December and most of us have thoughts of sitting up quietly, waiting patiently for the arrival of Christmas and the binges that it brings. Not so our rugby players. On Saturday 19 December those nice quiet people, the Italians, came to the Greenyards to take on the A team. In truth, this was no more than a full-scale warm-up for the coming Five Nations. It was absolutely a dummy run for what was perceived then as the number-one side, except that David Johnston, ex-Hearts foot-

Dominguez of Italy fails to stop Derek Stark

baller and Scotland centre, was to take charge of coaching matters instead of McGeechan. As it turned out this was nearly one of the most embarrassing days in Scottish rugby history as the Italians looked an impressive outfit and the Scots were made to look ordinary. Perhaps players certain of selection, like the Hastings boys, Chalmers and Armstrong, were saving themselves for bigger days to come and didn't relish the task in hand and all the risks involved. The trouble was they looked as though they were trying, while the pack found it hard to compete with the superior upper-body strength and better mauling technique of the aggressive Italians. It was best to put it down to an off day, although big Gavin, Duncan Paterson and David Johnston all admitted afterwards that the display had been appalling.

Bare statistics show that Scotland A won by 22–17, and the Scots felt that they were treated harshly in the line-outs where the Italians were penalised 26 times, exactly twice the Scottish figure, and should have been singled out more often by referee Ronnie McDowell from Ireland. 'Lies, damned lies and statistics' goes the quote, and it was only two late tries, from Derek Stark and Gregor Townsend, that pulled back the Italian lead.

On the plus side Derek Stark got the chance to show his pace on the wing, and most observers agreed that the hard core of the team, especially Gary Armstrong, Carl Hogg and Scott Hastings, had finished the game with no decrease in stature. But there were worrying signs that the side lacked mobility and strength. Perhaps it was proof of Italian rugby wanting to be taken seriously after domination of their domestic rugby by Antipodean imports.

Just to thumb a nose at the Scots, the Italians scored the last try of the game, rolling a maul relentlessly towards the Scottish line, Cario Checchenato touching the ball down.

A week later and the chance came for a redrafted side to take on their Irish counterparts in Dublin. Among other changes, Stirling County's aggressive winger-cum-full-back Kenny Logan was given a run in the number 15 jersey. Tony Stanger, Graham Sheil, and the excellent Andy Nicol came into the back division, while Alan Watt, now at loose-head prop, and Shade Munro were among the alterations in the pack. Rather strangely, the trial teams had been picked in advance, and it

Alan Watt on the move (Peter Kemp)

was Shade Munro who made that particular selection look odd with a stirring performance in the set piece and the loose. He was the only player in the side not to be involved too. Ian Morrison and Carl Hogg, again, both did themselves a world of good in Dublin.

Things weren't looking good with six minutes gone in the second half as the Scots trailed by 13–0. Andy Nicol got the show on the road with a try after positive lead-up work from Mark Appleson and a surging break by Munro. Next, Kenny Logan burst over from Nicol's short pass at the scrummage base, and Tony Stanger rounded off a remarkable comeback by the Scots with two late tries. The final score was 13–32 for the Scots.

One more game was to come on the agenda, and that the comprehensive defeat by the French on Scottish soil, but perhaps the less said the better.

Shade Munro seen here salvaging the ball for Glasgow against Edinburgh

Scotland v Italy

Scotland A v France A

Damian Cronin preparing for action

Rubislaw, Aberdeen, was the venue when the Scotland A side took on their French counterparts on Saturday, 20 March 1993. If the idea of playing the game in the North was to foster rugby, then it failed. The Scottish side performed poorly against an extravagant but workman-like French side and were in the end overwhelmed by five tries to one. The most depressing aspect of the game was the ease with which the visitors dominated the frontal exchanges and had they concentrated more on their rugby rather than the less acceptable aspects of their game, the margin would have been much greater.

Kenny Logan battered over for the Scottish try and Ally Donaldson added the conversion and four penalties, but the French scores, through Bertrank (two), and one apiece from Larran, Arbot and Galthie, re-emphasised the apparent strength in depth of French rugby. Conversions from Bellot and Labit were merely decorative in the scheme of the French victory, which was hardly the perfect way for the season to end for Scotland's mercurial second string which had battled hard to provide a medium for selectors and players alike to establish an accurate indicator of the merits of the Scottish game.

The A games in 1992–93 undoubtedly served the selectors' purpose in that they put players with potential on to a stage, and left it up to them whether they impressed or not. Carl Hogg, the Melrose back-row forward would have made the step up, but injury forced him from the scene, while those who were perceived to have found the going tough include Peter Jones, the Gloucester prop, Stuart Reid from Boroughmuir and veteran lock Chris Gray, whose season had been dogged by injury. Mark Appleson, the London Scottish winger, again indicated his talent which is suited to seven-a-side rugby, but seems restricted claustrophobically in the game of XVs. Italy's surprise performance was crucial in sorting out the Scottish XV's final make-up, and in that poor Scottish display much was learned about the Scottish squad's ability. That game, when we had sent out our national XV in the guise of an A side, more than any other in the season, gave the coaches and players in the full squad the resolve for the Five Nations that ensured another relatively successful season for rugby watchers at Murrayfield.

**The Royal Bank
of Scotland**

Travelling Hopefully on the Five Nations Trail

SCOTLAND'S 1993 CHAMPIONSHIP SEASON

Derek Douglas

To travel hopefully is a better thing than to arrive. It is not recorded whether Edinburgh's great man of letters, Robert Louis Stevenson, ever graced the green sward in pursuit of the oval ball but, without too much mangling to achieve the correct literary effect, his homily on the nature of life's journey can often be applied with equal truth to the annual pilgrimage along the Five Nations trail.

Gavin Hastings, Scotland's captain for the 1993 Championship campaign, is nothing if not a hopeful and optimistic traveller. During the week before Scotland's opening game against the Irish at Murrayfield, Gavin told anyone who would listen: 'I'm confident that we can really make an impact this season. In fact I would go so far as to predict that it's highly likely that we'll go to Twickenham in March with our sights set on, at least, the Triple Crown.'

Hastings, then with 41 caps and the northern hemisphere points-scoring record to his credit, had emerged as the obvious candidate for the captaincy following the retiral of David Sole after the 1992 Australian tour.

Hastings and Sole had made their international debuts together against the French in 1986. Since then the Watsonians full-back had become one of the team's 'senior pro's' and it came as no surprise when it was announced that he would skipper the side for the entire 1993 season.

Despite Gavin's optimism, most of those who follow the rugby saltire expected little from the season ahead. In the space of two seasons Scotland had lost Sole, Fin Calder, Derek White, John Jeffrey, Sean Lineen, Peter Dods and Iwan Tukalo. For a nation with such meagre rugby resources it seemed that the void of stellar proportions left by the departure of such a galaxy of stars would be just too much to overcome within the space of a single season.

Hastings and coach Ian McGeechan, who had intimated that it was to be his last Championship (certainly for the time being), never subscribed to the notion that the 1993 season should be one of consolidation, a period for taking stock and rebuilding. Outwardly at least, the shrewd rugby tactician that is McGeechan echoed the skipper and indicated that so far as he, too, was concerned it would be business as usual and that any talk of 'rebuilding' was negative and unwelcome.

But, in a literal sense, there had been rebuilding work going on elsewhere. At Murrayfield, the splendid new North and South stands were rising in all their concrete and steel glory from the terracings of recent and fond memory.

The builders were focusing on January 1993. The stands would be ready for the opening Five Nations game, The Royal Bank of Scotland International against the Irish, but for much of 1992 Murrayfield was out of bounds to all but the artisans who heaved and laboured over the physical manifestation of the foresight displayed by Scottish rugby's mandarins.

However, due to the transformation underway at Murrayfield, the international XV had been denied its traditional early

Opposite: *Derek Stark leaves Simon Geoghegan of Ireland flat on his face*

season workout. There were no visiting Argentinians or Romanians by which early pointers to form could be applied.

An unusually fine Inter-District Championship, with the South winning both the Championship and the right to tilt their lance at the All Blacks the following season, had, though, offered grounds for optimism. The Championship decider between the South and Edinburgh at the Greenyards during the second week in December had been particularly encouraging, not least because it indicated that the South's Gary Armstrong – missing because of injury from the 1992 Championship season – was back at the top of his considerable form.

A week after the Inter-District showdown, Melrose was once again the focus for Scotland's rugby élite as Scotland A turned out against Italy. This game, which the Scots were expected to win without much trouble, would give some indication as to just how the Scots would acquit themselves in the Five Nations Championship which was to get underway in three weeks' time.

And, in truth, the omens weren't good. The Scots stuttered along to a 22–17 win, only two tries in the final quarter overturning an Italian lead and restoring some semblance of respectability to the Scotland XV.

The game represented, too, an inauspicious debut for Hastings the captain. Never less than honest about his own performances Gavin said afterwards, with particular reference to his kicking of the ball from hand, that it had been 'appalling'. It was the utterly unconvincing nature of that Greenyards display which led some commentators and fans alike to look askance as, just a fortnight later – albeit with an A-team victory over Ireland by then under their belts – the skipper let it be known that he felt a Triple Crown could well be on the cards.

We know now, of course, that he was right. Scotland did travel to Twickenham with the Triple Crown in their sights but that wasn't how it looked to most people as the campaign got under way.

In retrospect did Gavin feel that he had been unduly optimistic? Had he allowed his 'hopeful traveller' tag to get the better of him? 'No. I was convinced at the outset that we could give a good account of ourselves and that we could go to

Twickenham with only the English to beat for the Triple Crown. I think you have to examine closely just what it was I was saying. We had Ireland and Wales at Murrayfield before we played the English and I was utterly convinced that we could beat them. I was saying that we would win our two home games.

'I had only lost two Murrayfield matches since I started in 1986 and these were both against England. There was no way that I could see the Welsh and Irish beating us on our own turf. That left the French. They were always going to be hard to beat in Paris but, so far as the Triple Crown went, I thought that it was a distinct possibility right from the outset.'

Speaking with the Five Nations dust long settled and in the midst of the Lions tour to New Zealand, Hastings emphasised, too, the marked difference between taking on the Italians at the Greenyards and the blood and thunder of a full-blown Five Nations campaign.

'Some folk obviously thought I was daft to be talking about the possibility of Triple Crowns so soon after a pretty poor display against the Italians but you have to remember that you really can't compare the two things. People were judging us on our performance against the Italians but once you get into the Five Nations, with big crowds and big stadia, then it's a completely different ball game. I was confident that we would improve.'

So, at Melrose in December, Scotland's finest turned out in A team guise but there was little doubt that the side bore a marked resemblance to what the selectors hoped would be, at least, the core selection for the looming Five Nations campaign.

Gavin Hastings was not alone in his condemnation of the side's performance that afternoon. Both coach David Johnston and team manager Duncan Paterson marked their charges' cards 'must do better'. Johnston, though, added with much truth that it was better to have got such a lacklustre performance out of the way against Italy rather than to have performed so badly against the Irish in three weeks' time.

One Scot who was able to rise above the general mediocrity was Derek Stark. The speedy Stark had been rejuvenated since transferring his allegiance to Boroughmuir. He appeared to have recovered from the psychological mauling inflicted upon him in a Scottish trial when last he had been on the verge of an international breakthrough. That doughty competitor Iwan Tukalo had psyched Stark out of the game and as a result the Kilmarnock chef's Scotland career had been put on hold. However, at the Greenyards Stark had augmented his undoubted pace (10.6 secs for the 100m) with a hunger for the ball and a ready answer for those who suspected that he had little liking for the game's ruder chores. He would be rewarded with a place in the side to meet the Irish at Murrayfield, and what a debut it would be.

Elsewhere, the selectors had been taking careful note of

Tony Stanger slips through the Irish defence to score a try

Hurry boys. Scotland v France

Robert James eludes Gary Armstrong

individual performances throughout the Inter-District Championship and the fruits of their labour would be there for all to see in The Royal Bank of Scotland International against Ireland.

One of those to prosper from some solid performances with the Exiles was the Bath lock Andy Reed. The 6' 7" Cornishman was undoubtedly the find of the season and he, too, would make his international debut against the Irish. Born of a Scottish mother and with Scottish grandparents, his Caledonian credentials would pass muster even among the most die-hard of traditionalists. Aged only 23, Reed's breakthrough into the international ranks had been rapid. Just a year beforehand he could not even call himself a Bath regular and yet there he was performing miracles at the line-out and contributing mightily in all phases of the international game.

He did not then, of course, know it but a Lions tour was still to come. By all accounts he did not have an entirely happy trip Down Under but he will have learned from the Kiwi experience and, with the aid of the Scotland back-room staff, will be encouraged to recognise the fact that he is an unusually gifted footballer who has the ability to lock horns with the best and play at the heart of the Scotland side for many years to come.

In addition to Reed, Scotland fielded another debutant forward for the encounter with the Irish. However, unlike the 'tenderfoot' Reed, even his best friends could not have accused Iain Morrison of being in the first flush of rugby youth. The London Scot flanker, a product of Glenalmond College and a Cambridge Blue, was 30 when he made his Scotland debut. However, and in this case just like Reed, he played as to the manner born and, at season's end, was unlucky not to have got the nod from the British Lions selectors.

Morrison's back-row colleagues were Hawick's Derek Turnbull, restored for his eleventh cap after a two-year absence, and Doddie Weir, the Melrose man filling the number 8 shirt for what, surely, is his natural international berth. Elsewhere in the forwards, Damian Cronin partnered Reed in the second row while Kenny Milne and Paul Burnell occupied their usual positions in the front row.

Which brings us to the problematical position of loose-head prop. Who was to fill David Sole's boots? That was the question which teased and tormented the selectors during their pre-season deliberations and, sadly, was to haunt them for much of the Five Nations campaign as well.

Gloucester's Peter Jones was the man in the number 1 shirt for the unconvincing display against the Italians. But he had been deputising for another Exile, the injured Alan Sharp of Bristol. Sharp had impressed throughout the Inter-District Championship and seemed the man most likely to attempt the impossible and pick up where Sole had left off. In rugby terms Sharp was a controversial choice, having previously been in the England camp to the extent that he even included a Sassenach B Cap in his rugby cv.

Nevertheless, Sharp was selected to play against Ireland and, indeed, joins that select band of players who actually appear in the match programme and yet fail to make it to the side. He had suffered a severe leg injury and, despite revolutionary treatment in a hyperbaric oxygen chamber, the fracture could not be coaxed into healing in time. One could feel nothing but sorrow for the luckless Sharp. It had been a bad break in more ways than one! However, his misfortune opened the door for another individual who has been no stranger to selectorial controversy.

The call went out to the 19-stone GHK man Alan Watt. Already converted by the national selectors from lock to tight-head prop, Wattie was now being asked to switch to the other side of the front row. More positions than the Kama Sutra? Not quite but in rugby terms certainly a roundabout route for a return to the national side. Watt acquitted himself well against the Irish where he provided the added bonus of his 6' 5" frame in the line-out. However, the loose-head jinx was to strike again and, as we shall see, Watt's re-emergence in the international arena would be brief indeed.

Behind the scrummage, the Old Firm of Gary Armstrong and Craig Chalmers were reunited at half-back. Armstrong, out for the 1992 season, had ousted Dundee's Andy Nicol to win back his place in the side. However, Nicol's time will come and it was always going to be the case that an injury-free and on-form Armstrong would win back his place, such is his stature as, arguably, the best scrum-half in the world. Gary's close-

No way through

Andrew Reed prevents Welsh rival Tony Copsey from gaining clean line-out possession

season decision to relinquish the number 9 jersey will sadden his many fans, but for Nicol it means that the opportunity to make the scrum-half berth his own comes sooner than expected.

With Stark on the left flank a rejuvenated Tony Stanger occupied the opposite wing and, between them, Scott Hastings was there to win his 43rd cap and, beside him, Graham Shiel had held off the challenge of the precociously talented but injured Gala youngster Gregor Townsend. That, then, was the side which accompanied Gavin Hastings on his journey down the 1993 Five Nations trail.

Saturday, 16 January dawned bright and breezy. As match time approached the winds grew even stronger until, at kick-off, a fairly respectable gale was swirling around the revamped Murrayfield stadium.

Because of the new North and South stands the wind characteristics were largely unknown to both sides. Goal kicking would become even more of a lottery than usual but to the credit of the Scots they were faster than their Irish opponents to come to terms with what was required both in kicking the ball from hand and in shots at goal.

The Irish skipper Michael Bradley won the toss and opted to play into what – in metereological terms – might be called the general direction of the wind. The flip of the coin itself is worthy of record, Hastings doing the honours and the Irishman calling. The Scotland skipper confided afterwards that so luxurious was the Cork man's brogue that neither he nor referee Ed Morrison had been entirely sure whether heads or tails had been called.

Scotland took almost immediate control and, with the 'official' line-out jumpers Reed and Cronin being augmented by the towering presence of both Watt and Weir, the Scots achieved a superiority on the touchline rarely seen by supporters of the men in blue.

Gavin Hastings kicked the Scots into a 3–0 lead with a penalty goal after three minutes and seven minutes later the debutant Stark made his mark on the game in a manner that is normally reserved only for the story books. It was *Boy's Own* stuff as the Boroughmuir winger sped over for a try with, literally, his first touch of the ball in international rugby.

From a Gary Armstrong tap penalty the ball was moved

out to the left via Milne, Turnbull and Reed. The Cornishman's pass was timed to perfection but Stark still had a bit to do and, in particular, he still had the tricky Simon Geoghegan to beat. Stark drew his man and then left the London Irish wing-three-quarter flat-footed. Hastings popped over the far from easy conversion and Scotland were ten points to the good.

The Scots continued to attack throughout the first half and just before the interval they struck again. Well-won ruck ball saw Chalmers and Scott Hastings through the gain line before Stark sent out a floated pass to Tony Stanger and the Hawick wing needed no second bidding to speed past the covering Richard Wallace and stride in for the try.

In the second period Scotland continued to play with great control and were rarely threatened by the Irish; the visitors' only points coming from Niall Malone who was credited with a penalty goal after four previous failures.

The final scoreline of 15–3 probably did little justice to the domination which the Scots had exerted but it was an encouraging start to the Championship campaign; the three new caps, Stark, Morrison and Reed, coming through with flying colours and Gary Armstrong proving that he had lost none of his devil through the injury-induced sabbatical.

For Armstrong, though, the game had an unfortunate legacy. We were not to know it at the time but the Jed-Forest scrum-half had picked up a nasty groin injury and he would play throughout the season only with the aid of pain killers. The injury never left him and it was eventually to be the reason for his unfortunate inability to take part in the Lions tour of New Zealand.

Meanwhile, at Twickenham the same afternoon, England, in pursuit of a unique third consecutive Grand Slam, were entertaining the French. And, just as the Duke of Wellington had declared after another tussle with the Tricolors, it was a damned close-run thing. Will Carling's men eventually scraped through 16–15 and even thus early in the season the Grand Slam challenge was very definitely in the balance. The game did, though, mark the emergence of two new talents: Ben Clarke, who would go on to be the player of the Lions tour in New Zealand, and Martin Johnson (called to the colours at 24 hours' notice to replace the injured Wade Dooley) served notice that they are going to be players of the first rank.

Back in Scotland preparations were in hand for the visit to Parc des Princes, the next port of call on the Five Nations trail. However, very soon, these preparations degenerated into something approaching French farce.

Bearing in mind the unusual manner of Alan Watt's arrival in the Scotland side which had just played Ireland – a game in which he had acquitted himself well – it was a savage irony that the genial giant should find himself on the sidelines due to illness.

Just a week before the Paris match Watt was playing in a club game against Watsonians at Myreside. He left the field late in the first half having suffered what had seemed to have been a run-of-the-mill knock on the ear. However, he did not return to the fray and it transpired that he was suffering from a viral condition. The following day it was announced that he was out of the French match and that the race was on to conjure up a replacement.

Alan Sharp had still not recovered from the hairline fracture to his left tibula and team manager Duncan Paterson announced that a decision would not be made until midweek, just days before the game. Grant Wilson of Boroughmuir and Gary Isaac of Gala were seen in many quarters as the likely candidates although it later transpired that the race had been between Isaac and another whom many had not even considered. The dark horse was Wilson's Meggetland clubmate Peter Wright. After much deliberation, and at the final hour, the selectors decided to gamble and ask the Boroughmuir blacksmith to switch from his usual tight-head berth (where he had won two caps in Australia the previous summer) to play on the left of the front row. It was a gamble that did not meet with universal acclaim but the selectors were ultimately proved correct. Wright made the transition without much difficulty and was rewarded with a Lions trip to New Zealand where, admittedly, he found the going somewhat harder.

Nevertheless, it was with Peter Wright now wearing the number 1 shirt that Scotland eventually took the field in Paris

Peter Wright in action against England

at a venue where they have yet to record their first international victory.

Sadly, that is a statistic which remains intact. The Scots went down 11–6 after failing to make the most of the scoring chances that came their way. In international rugby that is a vice which is met by condign punishment. Opportunities to put points on the board come so infrequently that if they are not taken then, invariably, all will be lost.

For much of the opening period Scotland had France on the back foot but aggressive defence by the Frenchmen kept the Scots at bay. Gavin Hastings had only one success from six penalty attempts although none of the kicks could be classified as easy. Didier Camberabero kicked two penalties from a similar number of attempts and at the end of 80 minutes the difference between the sides was a Thierry Lacroix try.

The Scots were down but not despondent. Ian McGeechan declared afterwards that in his opinion a Scottish side had never

Let me at them. Kenny Milne

played better at Parc des Princes; while Gavin Hastings, ruing those missed scoring opportunities, said that if they had played the same way again and taken their chances then the Scots would have ended up with a win and 20 points on the board.

On the same afternoon in Cardiff, England's Grand Slam hopes, dented against the French at Twickenham, were finally dashed in a 10–9 defeat by Wales. England's much-vaunted backs underperformed badly and the blame was placed on outside-half Rob Andrew. The 52-times capped Andrew became the ritual sacrifice as he was dropped for the first time in team manager Geoff Cooke's five-year reign. Into the side came Stuart Barnes, the Bath fly-half – who gives hope to pot-bellied rugby men everywhere – making his international return after five years in the wilderness.

Wales, who were to be Scotland's next opponents, made no change to their side and neither did the Scots. The Welsh came to Murrayfield for The Royal Bank of Scotland International

with confidence high after their narrow but supremely satisfying win over the English. However, their confidence was mis-
placed.

Scotland were in control of the game from start to finish,
the final scoreline of 20–0 doing little justice to the command
which the Scots had over the hitherto resurgent dragon. Once
again, just as it had done in the Ireland match, the wind swirling
around the new Murrayfield configuration proved problematical for both sides and, in fact, the Welsh skipper Ieuan Evans
admitted afterwards that when he won the toss he thought that
he had chosen to play with the wind at his back.

The game was notable, too, for the vociferous support
which the crowd gave to the Scots for the duration of the
proceedings. Against Ireland, perhaps adjusting to the new surroundings, the crowd had been strangely muted. But, against
the Welsh, and with their team in full cry, Scottish supporters
were in splendid voice and spontaneous outbursts of *Flower of
Scotland* were a feature throughout the entire 80 minutes.

Derek Turnbull scored the only try of the match after a
line-out drive and it was awarded in somewhat controversial
circumstances. The Hawick flanker was over the line with a pile
of bodies – friend and foe – on top of him. Joel Dume, the
French referee, confirmed his initial impression that a try had
indeed been scored by peeling off the bodies, layer by layer,
until Turnbull was revealed with a grin on his face and his
hands on the ball.

The remainder of Scotland's points came from the boot of
Gavin Hastings. Whereas the skipper had been wayward with
the speculative efforts in Parc des Princes three weeks earlier,
this time he mastered the tricky conditions to perfection and
was on target with the first five of eight attempts at goal.

At Lansdowne Road, the French were beating Ireland and
the race for the Championship – incidentally the first with a
new Five Nations trophy on offer – was still wide open. There
was, though, just one thought racing through Scottish minds.
Gavin had been right: 6 March was fast approaching and Scotland would, indeed, be travelling to Twickenham with the Triple
Crown in their sights.

But Twickenham has not been the happiest of hunting

grounds for Scots seeking Triple Crown glory. On eight previous occasions Scottish sides had gone south with just that one final hurdle to clear. But only in 1938, with Wilson Shaw at the helm, had high expectations been converted into reality. The 1993 vintage Scots fared no better than had most of their predecessors. Sadly, too, the match ended the Lions' hopes of Craig Chalmers, the Scottish fly-half sustaining a badly broken arm which sidelined him when selection for an outing with the tourists had been but a formality.

And if the aspirations of one outside-half ended in pain and despair, then for another the game represented the playing embodiment of five years of saying 'I told you so'. To Scotland's dismay, Stuart Barnes burst back into the international arena with a bravura performance.

Scotland's preparations had been hampered by a flu bug which had struck down the Hastings brothers, Andy Reed and Ian Corcoran the reserve hooker. In addition, Chalmers, Armstrong and Iain Morrison were carrying injuries, and the result was a restricted Murrayfield training session on the Sunday before the game – not the best preparation for the Twickenham trip where the Scots had not won for ten years.

England's eventual 26–12 win put paid to Scotland's Triple Crown hopes but for the opening 20 minutes the Scots had looked as if they might just have confounded the history books. Craig Chalmers had dropped a sweet goal to give his side a 6–3 lead when misfortune struck.

Chalmers went down and it was clear from the urgent note struck by England scrum-half Dewi Morris as he summoned assistance from the touchline that the injury was a bad one. The game was held up for nearly three minutes as, first the England full-back Jon Webb, a medic by profession, examined Chalmers's right forearm, and then the team doctor supervised the stricken Scot's departure on a stretcher. Chalmers went straight to hospital where surgeons inserted plates on the double-fracture injury.

Afterwards Craig said he had known straight away that the damage was severe: 'Gavin dropped the ball and I went down for it. The next thing I knew Dewi Morris was on top of me and I heard an awful snap. I knew right away what had happened.'

Derek Turnbull in possession against England

After the fly-half's departure Scotland's organisation seemed to go to pieces too, a fact acknowledged by Gary Armstrong who declared, 'Craig had taken a bit of stick from the critics and it's only when he's not there that you realise the contribution he makes. We lost our composure and by the time we had settled again England had the game won.'

Graham Shiel moved from inside-centre to the fly-half position and Gregor Townsend came on as a replacement to win his first cap. Thereafter England were in the driving seat. A Jerry Guscott try put England into the lead and Jon Webb added to an earlier penalty goal to make it 11–6.

Then Barnes set the game alight with a piece of impudent individualism which had Scots thanking their lucky stars that he had been ignored all these years. He evaded Morrison's attempt to shut him down and set off from inside his own half. He put Guscott into open space and Rory Underwood ran in for his 36th international try. The younger Underwood, Tony, scored a short time later and the boys' mum was caught by the TV cameras dancing a not so inscrutable jig in the stand. Jonathan Webb was on target with the conversion and the Scots had conceded 12 points within five minutes.

Gary goes ahead, supported by Iain Morrison

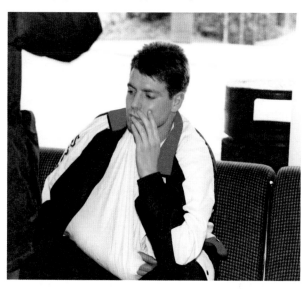

A thoughtful Craig Chalmers with his arm in a sling at Edinburgh airport
after the game with England

Thereafter the law of natural malice (which dictates that anything which can go wrong probably will) made a second appearance as the Scottish back division was dealt another blow. Scott Hastings departed injured and Tony Stanger moved to centre with Stirling County's Kenny Logan deputising on the wing.

Creditably, the much rejigged back line did not leak any further tries, the scoring thereafter being confined to a Webb penalty goal which was straddled by two from Gavin Hastings.

It may well have been the case that England were beginning to gain the upper hand just around the time that Chalmers was forced to leave the field but up until then the Scots had showed that they were intent on taking the game to the English and they had done so to good effect. For the Scots it was a melancholy manner on which to end the Championship season and scant reward for the priceless work done by Ian McGeechan whose last game it was.

Meanwhile, across at Cardiff Arms Park, where Wales were taking on Ireland, early season hopes of a revival for Welsh rugby were proving to be just another false dawn. And, similarly, any talk of the death of Irish rugby was – as Mark Twain put it – much exaggerated. Wales succumbed 14–19 to the fired-up Irish and a star was born. Eric Elwood, winning his first cap as Ireland's fifth fly-half in 12 months, kicked three penalty goals en route to Ireland's first Five Nations win since March 1990.

The Championship trail was nearing its end. By mid-March only England and France could win the new trophy. England travelled to Dublin to take on Ireland while the French entertained Wales in Paris. England fell at the final hurdle and, once again, Eric Elwood was the hero of the hour. The Lansdowne fly-half contributed a personal tally of two penalties and two dropped goals in a 17–3 win which had England on their knees by no-side. Elwood's performance had come too late to win him a seat on the Lions' plane to New Zealand but Mick Galwey, whose try was the source of the other Irish points, was rewarded with a place on the tour. So it was left to the French, with a flamboyant performance and a 26–10 victory on their own turf, to lift the new Five Nations trophy. It had been a long and hard road since January when the five hopefuls had set out on the Championship trail.

The final, and less often quoted, part of R. L. Stevenson's observation on the business of travelling hopefully and arrival reads like this '... and the true success is to labour'. On the Five Nations trail there was only one winner but along the way each and every one of the five contenders laboured. My, how they laboured. And that, as RLS rightly relates, is the true success of a Championship that continues to excite and enthrall and which continues to do so even in the face of an ever expanding and developing worldwide game.

FINAL TABLE

	P	W	D	L	F	A	Pts
France	4	3	0	1	73	35	6
Scotland	4	2	0	2	50	40	4
England	4	2	0	2	54	54	4
Ireland	4	2	0	2	45	53	4
Wales	4	1	0	3	34	74	2

Gregor Townsend

The Royal Bank of Scotland

Sevens Success Eludes Globe-trotting Scots

SCOTLAND'S WORLD SEVENS PREPARATION

Graham Law

The operettas of Gilbert and Sullivan would hardly spring read-ily to mind as a work of reference for one of the more fascinating aspects of Scottish rugby in the 1992–93 season. Yet a line from that engaging tale of Japanese nobility, *The Mikado*, seems rather apposite. 'Don't stint yourself, do it well,' is the instruction, among much conflicting advice, to the principal character.

That was the path on which the SRU embarked in the wake of the IRFB's decision to host the inaugural Rugby World Cup Sevens at Murrayfield. A Scot, Ned Haig, the Melrose butcher, after all, had given birth to the game some 110 years previously. Preparation for the three-day extravaganza in April was to be undertaken on an unprecedented scale. It entailed travelling to four continents in the space of five months in addition to specific sevens gatherings at Murrayfield. It also involved an outlay of some £71,000. Hindsight suggests the Union overdid it – though its motive always seemed reasonable to me – and some critics argued that sevens were attracting a disproportionate investment in both human and financial terms. The abbreviated game, they maintained, was supposed to be a bit of fun at the end of the season, not endless grind which eliminated innovation.

To be fair, however, there would have been no limit to the amount of opprobrious flak delivered in the SRU's direction if the Scots had flopped without taking advantage of the numerous tournaments where they could be exposed to the likely calibre of opposition they would face in the World Sevens. The Union had also been considerably chastened by Scotland's showing at the 1991 Hong Kong Sevens when, fielding a party consisting largely of Five Nations stalwarts – Scott Nichol and Ronnie Kirkpatrick were the only exceptions – they had lost to Canada in the quarter-finals.

The management for the World Sevens campaign were certainly not short of expertise in the quirks and nuances of the game. Led by Gala's Duncan Paterson with Douglas Morgan (Stewart's/Melville) and John Jeffrey (Kelso) acting as coaches, they knew the mixture of lung-bursting stamina, skill and aggression required to win a sevens medal. The trio were not helped by injuries. Looking back at the first squads chosen in July 1992 to participate in the autumn tournaments at Selkirk and Kelso, candidates such as Graham Agnew, the powerful, 26-year-old Glasgow High/Kelvinside winger, and international back-row forward Rob Wainwright had to withdraw through injuries which had not relented by the time the World Cup began. The injury to Agnew, the Rutherglen-based policeman, was particularly unfortunate. He sustained ligament damage in a tackle by Andy Nicol at the very end of a sevens squad session, just days after his pace had been seen to grand effect as Glasgow High/Kelvinside won their own sevens tournament. Indeed, when the World Cup Sevens kicked-off, the Scots' casualty list had lengthened to include Derek Stark, Tony Stanger, Kenny Milligan, Gary Armstrong, Brian Renwick and Iain Morrison.

Morgan consistently argued during the extensive travels, that if Scotland lost out to the innate brilliance of a Serevi, then there would be no disgrace. What neither he nor Paterson would condone, however, was dismissal through lack of effort. During the three-week tour in March 1993 which took in Australia, Fiji and Hong Kong, Morgan advocated that the hard slog on the training field – often conducted in the most alien of conditions – would prove 'money in the bank'. The evidence, however, suggested the players were overdrawn and had been pushed too hard. It struck me as more than coincidence that some two months later when Scotland returned to the South Pacific for a XV-a-side tour, there were no training sessions on Sundays when the players were permitted to unwind.

The opening salvoes in the sevens campaign were fired at the traditional curtain-raiser to the season – Selkirk – where Scotland and England were both among the guests. The latter departed in extra-time to a spirited Gala side – who will forget the tackle by the diminutive Grant Farquharson on the strapping Damian Hopley which saved the Borderers? – who went on to capture the tournament. Eight days later, Scotland's prospects looked a bit brighter when two SRU teams reached the final at Kelso, where the contribution of Doddie Weir in winning ball at restarts, an all-action showing by Kenny Milligan and some thumping work in both attack and defence by Ian Jardine were among the highlights.

Passports had to be readied thereafter, as in November Scotland set out for the Middle East, the United Arab Emirates to be exact, and the Dubai Sevens. Scots had ventured to this desert outpost before, yet for most of the party it was a novelty, especially playing on sand-packed pitches in baking heat. It required a last-gasp try by Derek Stark 90 seconds into stoppage time against the French Froggies to sustain Scotland's interest in the second day and as they retired to the tin hut which served as their dressing-room, one sensed much improvement would be needed come the dawn. It duly materialised, particularly in the first tie, the quarter-final against the holders, Queensland, who included the electrifying speed of Barry Lea and the silky skills of Brett Johnstone (subsequently capped by Australia as a replacement against Tonga during the summer).

Inspired by the London Scottish duo David Millard and Mark Appleson, the Scots trounced the Australians 28–5, setting up a semi-final against England. It was here that Gala's mercurial stand-off Gregor Townsend had one of his little brainstorms, only to redeem himself later in the tie. Townsend had retired to cover an English kick-ahead, reasoning that if he had got back, so, too, must some of his chums, when he caught out of the side of his eye what he reckoned was a fellow Scot. In fact, it was foe, the giant Bath forward, Martin Haag, who gleefully accepted the bounty of Townsend's pass to dot down a try, which helped England to a 12–7 interval advantage. Challenged about the incident that night, Townsend, as ever, remained unimpaired. 'You know how it is in the desert,' he volunteered, 'well, it was a mirage, wasn't it!' There was nothing imaginary, however, about his skill which brought the Scots level, nor about the strength of Millard who notched the decisive try which clinched a place in the final against Natal, whom Scotland eventually beat 22–12.

There was understandable jubilation at Scotland's success in Dubai but, perhaps, the view expressed by one experienced internationalist who was absent injured at the time – 'They did not really come across any of the big names in sevens' – was far from a case of sour grapes. What was encouraging, was that adverse circumstances had not stifled the Scots' chances. Indeed, for all that comparisons between sevens and XVs are invidious, the confidence which Derek Stark found on the sevens trip to the Gulf did not dissipate during the December A international against Italy or his Scotland debut against Ireland in January.

The focus over the next three months was rightly on XVs but the sevens squad still met regularly and 48 hours after Five Nations business was completed – when Triple Crown hopes had been dashed, yet again, at Twickenham – a ten-strong playing party, later to be reinforced by Andy Nicol, Derek Turnbull and Doddie Weir, departed on a three-week sevens tour encompassing tournaments in Australia, Fiji and Hong Kong.

The travel schedule was certainly unrelenting and, again, the management had little luck from the outset. Playing for Edinburgh Acads against London Scottish at Richmond on the morning of the Calcutta Cup game, Rob Wainwright (who had toiled all season with Achilles tendon problems but who had been named in the sevens pool as a replacement for Brian Renwick) suffered hamstring damage and had to withdraw. Wainwright's physique, pace and knowledge of the sevens craft, having repre-

Big Doddie Weir

sented the Penguins in Hong Kong in the past, were badly missed by the Scots. Problems of that ilk continued on the trip. Iain Morrison, the abrasive openside flanker who had a superb Five Nations campaign, could only play in Canberra, a knee injury eventually necessitating his return home for surgery to be replaced by Weir. A recurrence of a back problem forced Tony Stanger to miss out in Hong Kong, while Mark Appleson, Ian Corcoran, Derek Stark, Gregor Townsend, Murry Walker and Andy Nicol were all restricted by injuries at some point.

The tournament in Canberra was part of the capital city's 80th birthday festival and had to compete with a hot-air balloon show, a truckers' convention and an international wine-tasting (that's how the organisers described it) shindig. Twelve teams, split into pools of three, participated (in the sevens that is!) including the mighty Western Samoa and Fiji, Canada, the USA, Australia, and New Zealand provincial champions, Canterbury.

Scotland were installed as number one seeds – presumably as a consequence of the Dubai victory – and after posting a none too convincing win against Capital Territory of Australia in their opening game, seemed on course for a semi-final berth when leading Canada 14–5 early in the second-half after tries by Corcoran and Townsend. Thereafter, however, a series of self-inflicted wounds proved costly, the Canadians capitalising for a 26–14 margin. Scotland again missed chances before bowing out in the plate to Fiji, whose first-choice seven were engaged in domestic competition that day, though the Fijians themselves lost to Canterbury in the plate final and it was here that the Scots got a glimpse of the highly promising 21-year-old blindside flanker Todd Blackadder. The farmer with the size 15 boots made such an impression that he was eventually enlisted for the New Zealand squad for the World Cup Sevens at Murrayfield. Another engaging personality who used the Bruce Stadium as a stepping stone to the upper echelon was New South Wales's dashing utility back, Grant Lodge.

Both the finalists in the main competition, Canada and Samoa, had tackled tigerishly and showed a degree of physical confrontation which was a novel concept to most of the Scots

Opposite: *Chalmers fails to score from this penalty*

players in a sevens context. The Canadians, in truth, were not the Scots equals in pace and that weakness, allied to the innate ball-playing skills of the Samoans, inspired by Lolani Koko, helped the Pacific islanders to a 31–10 success and 23 tries in their four ties. That first-choice Samoan squad returned to training camp for the next week, in contrast to the Scots, Canadians and Americans – who were bound for Fiji and the inaugural international sevens tournament in Suva.

To most Fijians, XV-a-side rugby seems an irrelevance. Restrictions and inhibitions which mark the game's full version do not sit comfortably with their character. Their view of sport mirrors their attitude to life; it should be fun. Having endured the near four-hour bus trip from Nadi, in the west of the main island and the location of the international airport, the Scots set up base in Suva, which, during their preparation, lived up to its reputation for a wet climate. Anxious to avoid the showers which seemed to be triggered by Scotland's appearance at training grounds, manager Duncan Paterson had set out on an early morning jog only to turn on his heels when he was greeted by a rather long sea snake. Mythical serpents seemed to be conspiring against the Scots, as come the two-day tournament, featuring 16 teams, the temperature began to soar. Alas, it was not just a case of arriving at the ground one hour before kick-off. Determined to make a show of things, teams had to gather at a public park at 9.30 a.m. for a bus parade through the town centre during which offices and businesses simply closed. Then there was a Fijian welcoming ceremony (an excuse for the locals to dance and drink the mildly narcotic Kava?) – a bit like a common riding, perhaps, before the rugby eventually began some four hours later.

Scotland had no difficulties overcoming Vanuatu 40–0, running in six tries, but in the match which looked set to determine whether they would qualify, they lost 12–7 to Nadroga – Murry Walker's only outing during the entire three weeks. It did little to cheer the Scots that Nadroga went on to reach the all-Fijian semi-finals of the competition. The next day, sheltering in their changing-room (a tent) from the blistering heat, Scotland had to beat the Samoan development seven to maintain their interest in the main competition. For five minutes they monopolised possession but a breakthrough was denied and as the debilitating effects of the midday sun took their toll, the Samoans registered a 19–0 triumph. Derek Turnbull was so puggled by his efforts that he was unable to get enough breath to explain a shoulder injury, and it was a thoroughly demoralised Scotland seven who were sent reeling from the plate competition, missed tackles proving a millstone in their 38–5 exit to New Zealand.

Elsewhere, however, the quarter-finals were an all-Pacific affair fought out between Tonga, Samoa and six Fijian sides, including the national team who relied upon the brilliance of Waisale Serevi and finishing speed of Filimone Seru. The giant-striding Mesake Rasari was absent from the tournament through injury and it seemed inconceivable to Western eyes that the Fijians had already nominated their squad for Murrayfield, especially after the showing of the beanpole Nadi forward, Sailosi Nawavu, a centre in XVs, who, next to Serevi (nine tries and 91 points), had been the player of the tournament.

As the Fijians celebrated their victory as enthusiastically as the respective plate and bowl winners, New Zealand and Canada, Scotland were contemplating a gruelling speed endurance session beginning at 8.30 a.m. on the following day. At the time it struck one as some form of Presbyterian purge, though Morgan maintained it had always been in his plans. This is where some flexibility was needed. The players required recuperation, particularly as more travelling – by bus to Nadi and an early flight to Sydney, where they would stay overnight, before another early departure for Hong Kong – lay ahead.

In the colony, the Scots were billeted in the Hilton Hotel and trained on an adjacent pitch to the Fijians at Fort Stanley, base for the 1st Battalion Black Watch. It was too much to hope that some of the Fijians' intuitive flair would rub off on the squad for whom Derek Stark was returning to action after his groin problems had caused him to miss the Suva event.

Scotland's display at the two-day, 24-team tournament was an improvement on the previous fortnight, qualifying from their pool with victory over Romania (28–5) then a somewhat fraught passage against Tonga (10–7) where Corcoran's try was decisive. The Scots, though, still seemed somewhat shackled, unlike the exuberant Irish, who gave the Australians, Campese, Horan and

Little included, an almighty fright before going out in extra-time in the quarter-final.

Scotland took their bow at that juncture, too, vanquished 28–14 by Samoa, though as the player of the tournament, Lolani Koko, admitted it was a more testing tie for the Samoans than the scoreline suggested. Indeed, had Mark Appleson been able to latch on to a capriciously bouncing ball when the Scots led 7–0, then matters might have followed a different course. As it was, the Samoans were magnificent winners of the cup, blitzing New Zealand in the semi-final, then holding their nerve against an ill-disciplined Fijian side in the final.

The Scots' fate in the inaugural World Cup Sevens is detailed elsewhere in the book. Suffice to say that in restrospect the three-week tour placed too many demands on the players and left them with insufficient 'gas in the tanks' to do themselves justice at Murrayfield.

Scotland squad in Dubai – D. Stark, M. Walker (both Boroughmuir), M. Appleson (London Scottish), G. Townsend (Gala), D. Millard (London Scottish), C. Hogg (Melrose), I. Corcoran (captain) (Gala), A. Roxburgh (Kelso), I. Morrison (London Scottish).
Results – Scotland 12 Canada 12; Scotland 24 Orrell 12; Scotland 12 French Froggies 7. Quarter-final: Scotland 28 Queensland 5; Semi-final: England 17 Scotland 19. Final: Natal 12 Scotland 22.

Scotland squad on sevens tour to Australia, Fiji and Hong Kong – D. Stark, M. Walker (both Boroughmuir), A. Stanger (Hawick), G. Townsend, M. Dods (both Gala), M. Appleson (London Scottish), A. Nicol (Dundee HSFP), C. Hogg (Melrose), A. Roxburgh (Kelso), I. Corcoran (captain) (Gala), D. Turnbull (Hawick), I. Morrison (London Scottish) replaced by G. Weir (Melrose).
Results – Australia – Scotland 24 ACT 21; Scotland 14 Canada 26. Plate semi-final Scotland 0 Fiji 24.
Fiji – Scotland 40 Vanuatu 0; Scotland 7 Nadroga 12; Scotland 0 Western Samoa 19. Plate semi-final: New Zealand 38 Scotland 5. Hong Kong – Scotland 28 Romania 5; Scotland 10 Tonga 7. Quarter-final: Western Samoa 28 Scotland 14.

**The Royal Bank
of Scotland**

England Find Seventh Heaven

THE MURRAYFIELD WORLD SEVENS

Graham Law

Scotland's Ray Megson understandably did not look the suave, immaculate figure he cuts while earning his crust as a defence solicitor in the capital. Megson, the Edinburgh Wanderers referee, had required every ounce of his experience to keep the lid on an explosive final of the Hong Kong Sevens between Western Samoa and Fiji which he likened to tribal warfare.

As he left the field at the Government Stadium, the Samoans having been presented with the trophy after their richly deserved success, Megson echoed the sentiments of many rugby pundits at that time. 'It will be difficult to imagine the World Sevens at Murrayfield going to anything other than a southern hemisphere country. Scotland, at least, should benefit from having been exposed to their standard, but I rather think England could suffer from choosing not to play here.'

There were few dissenting voices. Yet some three weeks

Australia's Michael Lynagh has the measure of England's Chris Sheasby

Tim Rodber evades a Jim Fenwicke challenge to race in for England's third try against Australia

later, it was England's captain Andrew Harriman who collected the glittering 9ct gold Melrose Cup – gifted to the tournament organisers by the SRU – after a pulsating final against the game's XV-a-side world champions, Australia, a momentous achievement for a side who had eschewed elongated preparation and whose hierarchy gave the impression of being little more than lukewarm to the place of sevens at the game's top table.

In contrast to Scotland, Canada and the USA who had travelled the globe in an attempt to be in optimum shape for the World Sevens, England had played in just three warm-up tournaments: Selkirk, Harlequins and Dubai, though bear in mind their swotting prior to success in the SRU's Centenary Sevens in 1973 had consisted of a mere *one* training session.

In the Borders 19 years on, they had departed to eventual winners, Gala, in extra-time in the quarter-finals, though the trip to Philiphaugh was fruitful for Geoff Cooke and the England management, in that they saw the superlative contribution of Nick Beal, 21 at the time, who had joined the Franklins Gardens club only weeks before from Fourth Division High Wycombe.

He was duly rewarded with a place in the England squad for the Harlequins tournament which was sealed – in spite of defeat in their pool section by Cardiff – 38–14 against Newport in the final.

The sand-packed pitch of Dubai in November saw England suffer from injuries – Beal and the abrasive specialist sevens forward Chris Sheasby, who was diagnosed as concussed in the early rounds, were among the casualties – though there was still a battle royal against Scotland in the semi-final before the power of the London Scottish pair David Millard and Mark Appleson proved England's undoing.

Allied to that build-up was the early decision of the England top brass that their international thoroughbreds – the likes of Will Carling and Jeremy Guscott – would play no part in the festivities at Murrayfield as there were limits to the demands that could be placed upon them in a season which culminated in a Lions tour to New Zealand.

Thus when England disclosed their squad containing just two full caps – the army second lieutenant, number 8 Tim Rodber, and the majestic winger Harriman – there was a tendency for their prospects to be discounted, especially when they were drawn in a group comprising Western Samoa, Canada, Namibia, Spain and Hong Kong, from which only two would qualify for the main event.

Harriman acknowledged such pejorative comment was turned to the England team's advantage. 'What drove us on,' he confessed, 'was reading constantly in the press that we were a scratch side and that a lot of our Lions players were not going to be there. It needled us slightly. From adversity we found strength.' They also found no shortage of talent, a reminder once again to those on this side of Hadrian's Wall of the formidable depth of resources they have at their disposal.

Twenty-four teams arrived at Murrayfield on Friday 16 April. Capacity at the stadium was reduced to 37,500, with the West Stand off limits to the public and the wing stands demolished as part of the ongoing £41 million stadium redevelopment.

Holding a tournament of the calibre of the World Sevens on a partial building site posed problems for the event manager Charlie Bisset – a member of the SRU committee, who represented Scotland at swimming and won district honours for Edinburgh, Glasgow and North Midlands as a Heriot's lock. However, the reaction of participants – Australian captain Michael Lynagh was particularly effusive in his praise – to such concepts as the players' village illustrated that difficulties were not insurmountable.

For spectators, actual and potential, however, there were mixed tales. The vast majority of those who made it to Murrayfield did enjoy themselves during the 81 ties which were brought in exactly on schedule – a considerable coup – though many were frustrated by insufficient catering outlets. The question of how many more supporters, especially in the lead-up to the event, were dissuaded from pursuing tickets by the lack of information and poor marketing of a showpiece sporting occasion remains harder to quantify. The SRU, as long as seven months before the event, was doing its best, through the press, to keep the public informed about the inaugural competition and Bisset himself was readily available to deal with enquiries. The event, however, was the baby of Rugby World Cup Limited and marketing was its responsibility. As Bisset commented: 'The event was not promoted as well as it should have been in Scotland and certainly in the UK. I don't think promoting a tournament based in Edinburgh from London is the best way of doing it.' Ticket regulations, prohibiting sale on the day of play, were eventually relaxed after discussion with the police, but in spite of the attempts by the organisers to massage first-day attendance – they insisted it was 18,000, though there was no electronic means of checking whether the 18,000 tickets that had been sold for Friday were actually taken up – estimates from the emergency services put the figure at between seven and eight thousand.

No matter, Filimone Seru, the Fijian winger, had the honour of scoring the first try of the sevens as the South Pacific islanders defeated the tournament's minnows Latvia 42–0. That first day evolved slowly and by mid-afternoon desperately required a dash of the unexpected. Certainly, winger Paul Blom, 27, who

Derek Turnbull on the charge

England's delighted squad celebrate their victory over Australia

*Scotland's John Kerr holds off a challenge from Notoki of Japan to score a
try in the bowl final of the Murrayfield Sevens*

notched an early try, did his best before New Zealand eclipsed the Netherlands 49–7, while Ireland underlined French indifference to sevens with a 17–7 margin. Otherwise, however, it was predictably one-way traffic.

Enter 19th-seeded Tonga who, having lost to Scotland in their opening tie, were now awaiting pool favourites Australia. The Tongans had only been playing the abbreviated game since 1969 – it was introduced to the kingdom by an Englishman, John Pitman, and perhaps that association was to prove something of a talisman, considering the manner in which the cup was settled.

The Tongans, powerful and raw-boned, had won the plate in Hong Kong and proceeded to hand out a 10–7 defeat to the Wallabies. Isi Tu'ivai, a 22-year-old who plays for North Harbour in New Zealand, was their hero, claiming all their points through a try, conversion and drop-goal. 'I don't usually kick in XVs,' he said later, 'but the referee had said it was the last play of the game and the first thing that came to my mind was to go for the drop-goal.' The Australian coach Bob Dwyer was seething. He accused his players of being 'leaden-footed and appearing out of puff'.

The result ought to have proved something of an inspiration to Scotland considering the hosts had defeated Tonga 15–7 in their opening tie, courtesy of tries by Mark Moncrieff (2) and captain Millard. Yet in their next outing there was a distinct lack of ruthlessness and, sadly, an abundance of mistakes as Scotland lost 14–10 to Argentina, thus exacerbating the dogfight which qualification from their pool had become.

The Scots, Wallabies and Tongans all won their last match of the first day and were tied with Argentina at the top of the tightest qualification group. Elsewhere, Fiji and South Africa – the latter handsome 36–14 winners against Wales and for whom Andre Joubert, a full-back in the XV-a-side arena, had contributed 56 points overall – progressed serenely in Pool A. There was a similar tale for New Zealand and Ireland in Pool B, while England had managed 11 tries in their two ties against the Pool D small fry, an identical tally to Western Samoa who they were to meet on the second day.

The second day was not long in producing its first surprise

– the demise of the leg-weary Canadians 12–7 at the hands of Spain. Canada never recaptured the form they had displayed in the warm-up tournaments and did not live up to their reputation at Murrayfield. Scotland kept their qualification hopes afloat with a nervy 21–12 margin against Italy, who had actually led 12–7 at half-time, but there were ominous signs that Australia were moving into top gear as they blitzed the Pumas, and sure enough, a rather sorry Scotland, again missing too many tackles, suffered when they met the Australians in their last pool tie, where only a win would have ensured a place in the Melrose Cup quarter-final groups. The Scots' second-half rally, led by Haddington's John Kerr, who had performed creditably since his introduction for an out-of-sorts Gregor Townsend against Taiwan on the opening day, was too late as the hosts lost 26–14. Scotland, though tied on points with Argentina, finished fourth in their pool and were consigned to the bowl competition, an ignominious return from the investment which had been made during the extensive preparations at home and abroad.

There were conflicting assessments of Scotland's failure. One unpalatable suggestion was that we were lagging behind the rest of the world in both physique and skill. I would not subscribe entirely to that notion. The players who appeared at Murrayfield – with some honourable exceptions such as Kerr, Moncrieff and Ian Corcoran – did not do themselves justice and, later, were genuinely hurt by the perception that they had let down their country.

What might be closer to the truth is that – accepting the Scots' management were hamstrung by injuries to key players – those who remained were pushed over hard, especially at training during the three-week tour in March, and seemed incapable of exercising sufficient imagination to beat a defence by any other means than the kick ahead when they arrived at Murrayfield.

Fiji, many people's favourites to lift the honours, had shown signs of 'mental fatigue' early in the second day, all but passing up a 21–0 lead against Wales, who, courtesy of a brace of Simon Davies tries, recovered to 21–17. The cracks widened when the Fijians – persisting with players who were less than

Mark Moncrieff. Scotland v Japan

100 per cent fit, particularly Mesake Rasari, the huge hulk of a forward who was a pale shadow of the dynamic individual who had won player of the tournament at Hong Kong in 1992 – met the South Africans, relative novices to sevens, but not slow to grasp the essentials of the game. Sure enough, the South Africans, indebted to second-half tries by Ruben Kruger and Dieter Kriese, triumphed 26–19 to complete their pool matches unbeaten. New Zealand and Ireland were the qualifiers from Pool B, while Western Samoa and England – the former taking

the group match between the pair 28–10 – stepped up from Pool D.

Spectators who arrived a little late at the start of the third day's entertainment missed one of the major upsets. Ireland were relaxed and uncomplicated in their approach to sevens. Their players had had to be fished out of the Bull and Bear bar in Hong Kong in order to catch their flight home and that happy-go-lucky attitude – much more in keeping with the fun element supposed to be at the root of sevens – also served them well on the field. Their first opponents in the quarter-final pools were the Hong Kong champions, Western Samoa, and though the Pacific islanders had a number of players under the weather with flu symptoms, they would offer no excuses as Ireland, all hustle and bustle and in no way intimidated by their physical approach, stormed to a 17–0 win. Noel Murphy, their genial manager, instructed his charges chirpily from the touchline: 'Deep breaths now, lads,' and they certainly obliged, a gutsy success against Tonga ensuring passage to the semi-finals.

That match set the tone for a day of quality, quickfire

Appleson clears. Scotland v Tonga

sevens, something which had been missing – on a sustained basis, at any rate – during the opening two days. Harriman, Beal and Dave Scully were instrumental in the next tour de force, England's 21–12 margin against New Zealand. Samoa, after leading 12–0, were edged out 14–12 by Fiji, an exact reversal of the scoreline in the final at Hong Kong, and thus their interest in the tournament was ended. South Africa followed suit, though it had taken a courageous double tackle by Sheasby and the thrust of Damian Hopley in escaping the clutches of Chester Williams, to enable England to scrape past the Springboks 14–7.

New Zealand produced the most clinical demolition of the day (42–0) against Australia but then saw their path to greater glories obliterated by the South Africans, who saw no reason to soft pedal just because they appeared to be out of contention. A situation duly confirmed as Australia drew first blood against England to book their place in the semis where Fiji were to meet England and Ireland to face Australia.

England's tie turned on an incident – the tournament sponsors, The Famous Grouse, identified it as the finest moment of the three days – when David Scully, the 24-year-old uncapped Wakefield scrum-half, up-ended Rasari causing the ball to spill, Adedayo Adebayo exploiting the chance to send Harriman sprinting clear for the decisive try.

Ireland, cheered as if the North Channel had evaporated, had voluble encouragement from the crowd, the diligence of the speedy Richard Wallace – who finished the tournament with eight tries – and a willingness on the part of all to make the pulverising tackle, but as in Hong Kong, where the Wallabies had got the better of them, a missed conversion from Eric Elwood was to prove their undoing. Willie Ofahengaue's try, converted by Lynagh, saw Australia overturn a 14–19 deficit 15 seconds from time.

Before the final, Harriman, Cambridge graduate and prince in a Nigerian tribe, stressed to his team-mates that the Australians were certainly great players, yet, still, like other mere mortals, confronted by the mundane task of lacing up their boots. He needed no fear that his charges would suffer an inferiority complex and his confidence in his own searing acceleration –

simply too much for Campese and the 21-year-old Ryan Constable – set England en route to a 21–17 win, Lawrence Dallaglio and Rodber weighing in with the other tries before the Wallabies' fightback stemming from tries by Lynagh, Campese and Semi Taupeaafe.

Harriman, with a dozen tries in the tournament, was justifiably lauded for an imperious contribution. His pace, at which spectators had marvelled at Melrose in the colours of Harlequins in 1987, was unimpaired by the passing years. What prospect England defending their trophy? Well, the executive council of the International Rugby Football Board, meeting in Edinburgh later that week, delayed a decision on the future of the World Cup Sevens, but it would seem likely that if the event does continue it will be staged in Hong Kong, a tournament which has done so much to foster all that is best in the sevens game.

RWC Sevens: Final – England 21 Australia 17
England – Tries: Harriman, Dallaglio, Rodber. Conversions: Beal (3).
Australia – Tries: Lynagh, Campese, Taupeaafe. Conversion: Lynagh.
England – A. Harriman (captain), A. Adebayo, N. Beal, D. Scully, L. Dallaglio, C. Sheasby, T. Rodber. Rep: J. Cassell for Rodber. Also in squad: M. Dawson, D. Hopley.
Australia – D. Campese, R. Constable, M. Lynagh (captain), S. Taupeaffe, W. Ofahengaue, M. Burke, J. Fenwicke. Also in squad: I. Tabua, G. Lodge, J. Flett.

Bowl Final – Scotland 19 Japan 33. Plate Final – Argentina 19 Spain 12.

Scotland squad – M. Moncrieff (Gala), J. Kerr (Haddington), G. Townsend (Gala), M. Appleson, D. Millard (captain) (both London Scottish), A. Nicol (Dundee HSFP), C. Hogg (Melrose), I. Corcoran (Gala), D. Turnbull (Hawick), G. Weir (Melrose). Called up: S. Bennet (Kelso).

Kevin Amos (Jed-Forest) was deployed from the reserve squad for Romania and played in two games, scoring a try in his adopted country's 17–15 defeat by Japan.

**The Royal Bank
of Scotland**

Return to Paradise

SCOTLAND'S 1993 SOUTH PACIFIC TOUR

Graham Law

Last season's SRU president, Robin Charters, the former Hawick and Scotland centre, has first-hand knowledge of the many benefits overseas tours can bring the game here. Charters would be eager to admit that it was an amalgam of that admirable motive and the desire to journey off rugby's beaten track which prompted him, as a member of the Union's committee in the 1980s, to suggest that a gap in Scotland's tour schedule in 1993 could be filled with a trip to the South Pacific. 'It was only after the committee had agreed,' he recalled cheerily, 'that a few of them worked out that I would be president that year and it would be a nice wee trip for me too!'

Thus, last May and June, Scotland embarked on a seven-match development tour to Fiji, Tonga and Western Samoa. Prior to the off, there were so many imponderables surrounding the venture, not least how players, by the selectors' own admission sometimes ranked as lowly as fifth in the Scottish pecking order, would fare against opponents renowned for their abrasive physical engagement and natural tendency to give flair its head. Indeed, as Scotland's tour coach David Johnston affirmed: 'People did not believe that players down the pecking order, generally ranked from 20–50 in Scotland, would be up to this trip.' On return, however, the tour had to go down as one of the most successful ever undertaken and certainly the happiest such odyssey since the unbeaten expedition to Zimbabwe in 1988.

Much of the credit for that had to go to the management team – coach Johnston, his assistant Richie Dixon, doctor Jimmy Hay, physiotherapist David McLean and manager's assistant Arthur Hastie – ably led by the former international referee Allan Hosie. A lucid communicator and thoroughly adept at man-management, Hosie also proved something of a sooth-sayer. Before departure the manager had observed: 'The net is being cast wider than normal. Having said that, that's no bad thing. If we can get a percentage of these boys through this, it might give us a wider base than we currently have, where I feel we are asking too much of too little.'

Whether Hosie had individuals in mind when he made that remark is a moot point. The upshot of the tour, however, was that the likes of Bryan Redpath, the 21-year-old Melrose scrum-half, Murray Wallace, the 25-year-old Glasgow High/ Kelvinside flanker and Rob MacNaughton, 27, the Northampton centre, personified Hosie's vision. Much was known beforehand about the merits of Gregor Townsend (Gala). Ian Jardine (Stirling County), Shade Munro (GHK), David McIvor (Edinburgh Acads) and Carl Hogg (Melrose). For them the tour marked another rung on the ladder to the rugby firmament. But the unsung trio I have listed proved during the five weeks that they are worth rather more than places among the cannon-fodder at Murrayfield squad sessions. To that short leet one might also add the Gala prop Gary Isaac who, particularly in the Test against Tonga, had a formidable tour.

For a party, which during the course of the tour swelled to 32 players – only 12 of them were internationalists with a total of 75 caps among them – to emerge with six wins out of the seven games, surpassed all expectations. Therefore, it saddened me that there was some petty sniping at home, belittling the standard of the opposition and questioning whether everything would have gone so swimmingly in terms of morale had results been different. Such views were ill-founded. Of course there was still concern that Scotland's backs were not making more creative use of a multitude of possession – a problem inherited from last season's Five Nations campaign and on which Johnston especially has firm thoughts. Yet the fact that around 20 of Scotland's front-line players had been unavailable for the trip – through a combination of the British Lions tour of New Zealand, injuries and domestic and personal commitments – and that only Doddie Weir from the Five Nations regulars was among the party, served to underline the magnitude of what was achieved.

Two days before the squad left, Weir was among the Scots struggling with an unseasonal snowfall on his family's hill farm at Cortleferry near Stow in the Borders. On arrival in Fiji after a 34-hour journey from Edinburgh – via London, Los Angeles and Honolulu – the temperature was in the 80s.

The journey was not without mishap. Tour captain Andy Nicol – who had sustained a blow to his knee during the Alloa Brewery Cup final won by his Dundee HSFP club against Edinburgh Acads earlier in the month – was stretching out during the first leg of the flight to LA when one of the stewardesses – watch out for her when you are doing your shopping – guided a drinks trolley into his injured leg. Scotland's scrum-half needed ultrasound treatment and though he did most of the training on arrival, he was left out of the team for the first match against Fiji B in Nadi as a precaution.

The party soon began their assimilation into life Fijian style. The country's prime minister, Sitiveni Rabuka, joined them, unheralded, in their hotel restaurant for breakfast – without a security guard in sight. To Western eyes it was akin to John Major turning up at the local Post House and joining the vegetable queue with company who had not been positively vetted. The press – ever vigilant – made mental note that attendance at the Edinburgh Acads v Gala match this season would make interesting viewing after David McIvor (plus camera) was bundled into the hotel pool by Gary Isaac, while coach Johnston

Scotland v Tonga. Murrayfield Sevens

digested the news that his charges would be playing under the newly amended laws during the tour.

The SRU's insistence that all games were handled by neutral referees was a godsend – the referees in Suva actually took 'strike action' during the Scots' stay on Fiji – and Johnston and Dixon were both vindicated in their belief that the new requirement in the laws for players joining the maul/ruck to do so behind the hindmost man, would be to Scotland's advantage. Both coaches had been in harness on the national tour to Australia 12 months previously where the first port of call was Darwin. The perception that some of the younger players then were intoxicated by the idyllic surroundings meant that rugby was pre-eminent in their approach in Nadi. Following the practice of recent tours the management decreed that all players, injury permitting, would be fielded in the first two games, a scenario which duly unfolded.

The opening match was played in torrential rain and intense humidity which did not excuse the meagre return the Scots garnered from a period of around one hour's control of both position and possession. Jet lag and the long period of XV-a-side inactivity for many of the team were added as a plea in mitigation. They were forced to defend tenaciously in the last quarter as they held on to a 14–7 advantage and were indebted to Haddington winger John Kerr's try-saving tackle on his opposite number and Weir's grounding of the Fijian number 8 and Test veteran Timoci Wainiqolo. Johnston knew the defeat in the first match in Australia had proved to be a millstone, and he was heartened by the result. 'Over the piece the backs played conservatively and got a conservative win,' he mused. 'We can play in a more expansive fashion given the conditions and another few days just to bed into the tour.'

The following day the Scots made the four-hour coach trip to the island's capital, Suva, a rather unappealing, grey port which did not fit the image of a tropical paradise. Even had they been staying put in Nadi, however, the management had decided that Sundays would be free of training, a decision the players were to appreciate as the tour progressed. Training at the match venue, the Commonwealth Stadium, the Scots were

Carl Hogg

95

told a state-of-the-art scrummaging machine had been installed. It might as well have been a Heath Robinson affair, however, as the New Zealand-manufactured machine had not been properly secured and was lying open to the elements. None of the locals appeared to know how to programme the hydraulics either, thus assistant coach Dixon was pressed into service as mechanic/tutor. 'It's a bit like driving a JCB,' he enlightened the press, betraying the joys of childhood on a Berwickshire farm.

The 51–3 success (eight tries to nil) which followed against Fiji Juniors had elements of the bulldozer about it as the Scottish pack ran their naïve opponents ragged. Aside, however, from some silken skills from Andy Nicol at scrum-half and Scott Nichol at outside-centre, there was general disappointment in the display by the backs. Nick Grecian's goal-kicking was as awry as Ally Donaldson's had been in Nadi and Gregor Townsend failed to stamp any sort of authority on proceedings from stand-off.

The build-up was now underway for the Test but the Fiji Rugby Union made no effort to promote the game and consequently attendance on a blustery Saturday when the temperature dipped below the 70s was at best 1,500. The Union seemed belatedly to have awakened to the demise of interest in the XV-a-side game in a country where sevens are held in higher esteem. The helter-skelter style of play associated with sevens seemed prevalent in many of the XVs matches we saw, although the national team, coached by Esala Teleni, the former number 8 who toured the UK in 1982 and 1989 and also represented both British and Welsh Universities, were more inclined to probe around the fringes and mix up their approach. Scotland had opted mostly for experience for the Fiji Test and it was impossible not to feel sympathy for Munro, Hogg and Wallace who had all made sterling contributions to the midweek game only to miss out to the seasoned trio of Chris Gray, McIvor and Ian Smith. Gray again had problems in the line-out – where Robb Scott was his boilerhouse partner – but scrummaged soundly and was very much in the van with McIvor and Hawick hooker Jim Hay in the loose where the Scottish pack drove superbly in the final quarter to steady nerves after Fiji had levelled at 10–10. Kenny Logan had a rollercoaster day at full-back, spilling four passes as he entered the line and looking giddy under the high ball when Scotland played against the wind in the second-half, yet redeeming himself with a try-saving tackle on Tomasi Lovo. There was again concern about the goal-kicking, Ally Donaldson managing only four kicks from 11 attempts and, in the first-half especially, Donaldson too often surrendered the initiative by opting to kick rather than pass.

Assistant coach Dixon felt the problem, as the tour progressed, would be for the forwards to continue presenting the quality of possession they had achieved to date. He remained convinced that the backs would improve. His conviction was probably strengthened by a long chat he had prior to the Fiji Test with Gregor Townsend, whose miserable experience during the World Cup Sevens and the fact he had not played stand-off in XVs since the end of February had dented his confidence. Dixon, however, told the Edinburgh University student to put it all behind him and that the tour management believed he had a grand future at stand-off.

Townsend justified that confidence when the Scots arrived in Tonga – the kingdom cluster of 170 islands less than 40 of which are inhabited. A row had been bubbling prior to the Scots' arrival. The kingdom's police minister, who in the quaint world of South Pacific politics doubled as the official hangman, had ruled that policemen could not represent the national rugby team after a match between the police and a local team had been abandoned due to foul play, the official Tongan RFU inquiry attributing the bulk of the blame to the police. Six policemen were in the Tonga national squad and it took the intervention of the country's sports-mad monarch, 75-year-old King Taufa'ahau Tupou IV, to have the sanction lifted in time for the two matches the Scots played. The king's favourite pastime is rowing but he attended the Test match involving the Scots and allowed them to use his personal scrummaging machine – in contrast to Fiji it was properly maintained and obviously in regular use – and call in at the superb gym which he patronised adjacent to the match venue, the Teufaiva Stadium.

Victory in their first match in Tonga – against a President's XV which contained seven of the side who were scheduled for Test duty – was, in my view, the most satisfying result of the tour given its development status. The 21–5 margin was built around polished tactical control from Townsend, some indefatigable work in attack and defence by the back row of Kevin Armstrong, Hogg and Wallace, and the balance and poise of Rob MacNaughton in the centre. MacNaughton, an architect whose projects during the tour included renovation on the Althorp estate, family home of the Princess of Wales, could soon be meeting another member of the royal family if he maintains the rich impression he made in the summer. Sadly, however, he suffered shoulder damage in the match which was far more physical than anything the Scots had encountered in Fiji. He was not the lone casualty as both Martin Scott (back) and Kenny Milligan (calf) also had to retire and were soon bound for home replaced by Ian Corcoran (Gala) and Cameron Glasgow (Heriot's).

The Test saw the Scots' scrummage at its most potent and it was no surprise a pushover try was claimed – one of six the Scots registered during the tour. Yet the menace in that phase was not matched in others, a worry, with the Samoan leg of the tour on the horizon. The 23–5 triumph saw another combative performance from Ian Jardine, whose fearsome tackling had earned him the nickname of 'Axeman' from his fellow players.

Scotland then crossed the dateline, an unnerving experience, leaving Tonga on the Tuesday night and, after a one-hour flight, arriving in Samoa on the Monday night. 'I haven't had a drink since tomorrow,' quipped a somewhat bemused Robin Charters.

The party's hotel – Aggie Grey's – was a considerable improvement on their base in Tonga and the players learned that the legendary Hollywood star Gary Cooper had stayed there when filming the epic *Return to Paradise* in the 1950s.

Kevin Armstrong was unable to travel on to Samoa, a back injury he had sustained in training forcing him to return home. There were more injury problems after the midweek 33–8 victory over a Samoan President's XV, too, Carl Hogg having to travel to New Zealand for surgery on his broken nose, the damage sustained from a vicious forearm smash by the hosts' teenage scrum-half who was rightly sent off and received an eight-week suspension. Hogg was ruled out of Test selection –

I remain convinced he would have been promoted – while his Greenyards colleague, Bryan Redpath, he of the fast and long service, was also *hors de combat*, a back injury preventing him from replacement duty for the Test.

I was a little disappointed the selectors had not gone for broke in the final game and exposed more players to yet a higher level. MacNaughton (perhaps out of a desire to protect his shoulder) was missed in midfield where Scott Nichol's light-weight frame was too easily shrugged aside by the powerhouse physiques of the Samoans, while Smith seemed jaded in the back row and Mark Moncrieff and Logan out-of-sorts on the wing. The gamble of selecting Grecian at full-back – after a far from convincing outing in that berth in the midweek game – did not backfire, while if other Scots had displayed the defensive steel of Jardine, the result might not have been as damning as a 28–11 defeat, albeit only 3–1 on the try count. Speaking to the Samoan players afterwards there was incredulity that Jardine was not a full cap. 'You're kidding,' said scrum-half Junior Tonu'u, a man the All Blacks are showing more than passing interest in. 'That guy would be ideal to face New Zealand.'

The tour's 100 per cent record had been dashed at the last, yet nevertheless, Johnston was spot on in my book to proclaim the tour a success. There was no hyperbole either when he said every single player had made improvements during the venture. The bonus for Scottish rugby will come over the next two seasons.

Tour party: Backs – N. Grecian (London Scottish), A. Donaldson (Currie), I. Jardine (Stirling Co.), J. Kerr (Haddington), K. Logan (Stirling Co.). R. MacNaughton (Northampton), B. Redpath (Melrose), K. Milligan (Stewart's/Melville) replaced by C. Glasgow (Heriot's), S. Nichol (Selkirk), A. Nicol, captain (Dundee HSFP), C. Redpath (Melrose), G. Townsend, M. Moncrieff (both Gala), D. Wyllie (Stewart's/Melville).

Forwards – K. Armstrong (Jed-Forest), S. Ferguson (Peebles), C. Gray (Nottingham), J. Hay (Hawick). C. Hogg (Melrose), G. Isaac (Gala), A. Macdonald (Heriot's), M. Wallace (GHK), D. McIvor, (Edinburgh Acads), S. Munro (GHK), M. Scott (Edinburgh Acads) replaced by I. Corcoran (Gala), R. Scott

(London Scottish), I. Smith (Gloucester), G. Weir (Melrose), G. Wilson (Boroughmuir) P. Jones (Gloucester).

Results: Scotland 14 Fiji B 7. Scotland scorers: Try – Kerr. Penalties – Donaldson (3). Scotland 51 Fiji Juniors 3. Scotland scorers: Tries – Hogg (3), Nicol (2), Wallace (2), Grecian. Conversions – Grecian (4). Penalty – Grecian. Scotland 21 Fiji 10. Scotland scorers: Tries – Hay, Logan. Conversion – Donaldson. Penalties – Donaldson (3). Scotland 21 Tonga President's XV 5. Scotland scorers: Tries – Townsend, Penalty try. Conversion – Townsend. Penalties – Townsend (3). Scotland 23 Tonga 5. Scotland scorers: Tries – Penalty try, Weir, Logan. Conversion – Townsend. Penalties – Townsend (2). Scotland 33 Western Samoa President's XV 8. Scotland scorers: Tries – Penalty try, Gray, Weir, Nicol, Kerr. Conversion – Donaldson. Penalty – Donaldson. Drop-goal Wyllie. Scotland 11 Western Samoa 28. Scotland scorers: Try – Nicol. Penalties – Townsend (2).

**The Royal Bank
of Scotland**

The Lions Beaten but Untamed

THE 1993 LIONS IN
NEW ZEALAND

Bill McMurtrie

Gavin Hastings and his 1993 Lions were agonisingly close to fame. They recovered so well from the loss of the first Test in Christchurch that they squared the series by registering a record 20–7 win against the All Blacks in Wellington. Inevitably, memories were evoked of the Lions' comeback to win the 1989 series against the Wallabies after the loss of the first Test, but Hastings was not to emulate his fellow Scot, Finlay Calder, captain in Australia four years earlier. The All Blacks, wounded by the Lions' biggest Test victory in New Zealand, came back to win the decider in Auckland by 30–13.

Nor was another Scot, Ian McGeechan, to achieve the ultimate as Lions coach in 1989 and 1993. He departed from international rugby without the series victory against the All Blacks that had eluded him as both player and coach.

Yet the pattern of the 1993 series would have been so differ-

A relaxed Gavin Hastings

ent if the first Test had been only a couple of minutes shorter. Grant Fox's late goal from a debatable penalty snatched a 20–18 victory for the All Blacks. The two other Tests were much more decisive – one each way.

Memories of the tour also would have been different if the first Test had not been cruelly plucked from the Lions' grasp. The provincial results, if not forgotten, would have featured with less emphasis in the final analysis of the tour.

Instead, the Lions will be remembered as having the worst playing record of any team representing the British Isles on tour. Little better than breaking even, they played 13, won 7, lost 6. In addition to the Test series the Lions' wins against North Auckland, North Harbour, the Maoris, Canterbury, Southland, and Taranaki were offset by defeats by Otago, Auckland, Hawke's Bay, and Waikato. The last of those was by the humbling margin of 38–10, the heaviest defeat suffered by any Lions team against a New Zealand province. Also, in the try-

Kenny Milne in serious mood

scoring count over the tour the Lions had only a fractional advantage, 33 against 31.

It was an unfair tour schedule that sent the Lions in against Waikato in the midweek between the second and third Tests. The Lions, like any touring team, would have preferred a less demanding game at that stage whereas Waikato, as New Zealand champions, merited a Saturday match. Such refinements in scheduling, however, are less practical the shorter the tour because of the inevitably tighter financial budgeting imposed on the host union, and though the 1983 Lions in New Zealand had two or three easy runs in their 18 matches their 1993 counterparts had to accept that they would have to meet mainly first-division opposition when only ten non-Test games were to be played.

Yet anyone who was on the tour, whether participating or following, could surely not subscribe to the pessimists' view that such ventures are now archaic. British Isles tours may necessarily be less frequent than before because of the pressure that the World Cup imposes on space in the international rugby calendar, but waiting for the Lions makes the heart grow fonder. According to the International Rugby Football Board's tour schedule, it will be 12 years before the Lions return to New Zealand. That is longer than the top-level lifetime of all but exceptional players. Yet to play for even a provincial team against the Lions is a young New Zealander's dream, and it was consequently little wonder that even less rated teams were fired up against the tourists. Otago put a dismal Super Ten series behind them in beating the Lions 37–24, but it was Hawke's Bay who caused the greatest upset in coming from behind for a 29–17 victory.

Hastings emerged from the tour with great credit as captain – an inspiration on the field, a diplomat and a gentleman off it. The Scottish full-back set an example that readily bonded the nations, even when the Test teams were dominated by Englishmen, and even though he was the only Scot in the XV for the second match of the series his charisma and presence were crucial in the Lions' victory. No one appeared unsettled when a Hastings fumble conceded an early try to Eroni Clarke: all of his fellow Lions had genuine belief that the captain himself would not allow such a momentary lapse to upset him.

His younger brother, Scott, was accelerating fast towards his best rugby in his first couple of matches. The centre's game was stirring memories of his 1990 Grand Slam form and earlier days, but suddenly he was removed from the tour by a severe fracture of his left cheekbone during the Dunedin match in which Otago beat the Lions. The damage was such that the broken bone had to be screwed together in a four-hour operation and his mouth had to be temporarily restrained by elastic bands to prevent excessive movement.

Three other Scots, Paul Burnell, Kenny Milne, and Andy Reed, played in the first Test, making up the pack's front five with Martin Bayfield, the giant English lock, and Nick Popplewell, the popular Irish prop. After the Christchurch defeat, however, all three Scottish forwards were dropped, joining two compatriots, Peter Wright and Damian Cronin, on the sidelines, and so Gavin Hastings was left as the lone Scot in the Test team.

Burnell and Milne especially did not deserve to be scapegoats for defeat, but they had to give way to two English forwards, Jason Leonard and Brian Moore. The London Scottish prop and the Heriot's hooker themselves were justifiably convinced that they would have remained in the Test XV if the Lions had won the Christchurch international.

Each appeared to be a change for the sake of change. Neither Leonard nor Moore had obviously been superior to his Scottish rival in any one phase of the game. Leonard even had to switch from left to right prop to displace Burnell, a move that was first hinted at when the Lions played against Taranaki at New Plymouth in the midweek after the first Test. The tourists had a comfortable win by 49–25, and even though Leonard was not tested he remained for the Saturday match against Auckland at Eden Park. Despite the Lions' 23–18 defeat in that game Leonard stayed on in the Saturday team for the two remaining Tests whereas Burnell, like Milne, was in the XVs beaten by Hawke's Bay and Waikato.

Neither Burnell nor Milne could rise above the general slough of despondency in those two defeats. They were not alone, however, and the inevitable thought dwelled in the touchline mind that Leonard and Moore could hardly have fared better had the boots been on the other feet, with the Scottish pair still in the Test team. McGeechan, as a tour selector, was party to the three Scots' omission from the Test team, but he acknowledged that Burnell and Milne especially were unfortunate to be dropped. It was consolation, however small, for that pair when the coach remarked that they had had 'a good tour'. They would, of course, have had a happier tour if that commendation had been backed up with Test places throughout the series.

Reed, the third Scot omitted after the first Test, gave way to Martin Johnson, the English lock who had been drafted into the tour after Wade Dooley had gone home because of his father's death. Yet the Anglo-Scot from Bath had done enough to force the New Zealand selectors to omit Ian Jones after Christchurch, and if Reed could take any consolation from his brief career in the Lions' Test team it would be that he had come a long way in his first half-year of international rugby – from his debut for Scotland against Ireland at Murrayfield in January to the Lancaster Park Test in June.

Neither of Scotland's other tight forwards, Cronin and Wright, aspired to the Test team. Indeed, the tour's benefit for Wright was to sway him towards considering loose-head as his more permanent position in rugby. Throughout his Borough-muir career Wright had been a tight-head, though dabbling in experience on the other side of the front row in practice at Meggetland. His two caps on Scotland's 1992 tour to Australia – which Burnell missed because of injury – also were at tight-head, and though he played in three of Scotland's 1993 inter-national championship matches as left prop he went with the Lions to New Zealand in his established position. Only when Leonard switched to tight-head for the Lions did Wright move over for three games on the left. It was enough to persuade the Boroughmuir prop to think seriously about playing more regularly on the left, especially as his Boroughmuir colleague, Grant Wilson, had been on Scotland's South Pacific tour as right prop even though more practised at loose-head.

Two other Scots would have been on the tour but for injury. Gary Armstrong was in the original squad, though dropping out less than a month before the Lions' departure from home, whereas his international half-back partner, Craig Chalmers, was ruled out of contention when his right forearm was broken during Scotland's Twickenham match against England two days before the tour selection was announced in March.

Armstrong was much missed by the Lions. Neither Dewi Morris nor Robert Jones had the amalgam of the Jed-Forest scrum-half's hard-bitten competitiveness, service security, and general astuteness. Morris hinted at what might have been when he played well above his tour form during the Lions' victory in the Wellington Test. Yet Andy Nicol's six minutes of Lions rugby were enough of a reminder of what the Lions were missing. Nicol, Armstrong's understudy for Scotland for the past two years, was called over to New Zealand from Western Samoa at the end of Scotland's South Pacific tour as he was needed as emergency cover when Jones developed a throat infection on the weekend of the first Test. Jones played in the next match, when the Lions beat Taranaki 49–25 in New

Paul Burnell

Plymouth, but an arm injury to the Welsh scrum-half allowed Nicol those few minutes to state emphatically that Scotland had the best two scrum-halves in British rugby. The Dundee High School FP scrum-half, who had been Scotland's tour captain, was truly a Lion even though he had to borrow Ian McGeechan's blazer to look the part off the field.

The New Plymouth result was the best the Lions had in the ten non-Test games. Ironically, though, their only win in five games thereafter was in the second Test. By then the tour squad had been defined into the Test team and the also-rans, and unfortunately the latter group did not function as a unit. No one emerged to lead them on the field, no one content to do his bit as midweek captain. The 1989 Lions had Donal Lenihan, and the 1990 Scots in New Zealand had Alex Brewster. Donal's Donuts and Brewster's Beezers became almost as crucial to their tours as the respective Test teams.

It was a handicap, too, that no one emerged as the obvious back-up for Peter Winterbottom as open-side flanker. When Winterbottom was rested Richie Webster shouldered the responsibility more often than not, though without looking the part, especially when he had to stand comparison with the likes of Waikato's Duane Monkley. Ben Clarke shaped up in his one game at open side, when the Lions beat Canterbury 28–10, but invariably he was needed elsewhere, especially as blind side in the first-choice back row beside his English colleagues, Dean Richards and Winterbottom.

Yet the early games on the tour gave no hint of troubles to follow. The Lions opened with a 30–17 win over North Auckland in Whangerei, they followed up by beating North Harbour 29–13 at Auckland's Mount Smart Stadium in the only tour match that seriously boiled over, and the tourists then came from 20 points down in beating the Maoris 24–20 at Athletic Park, Wellington. Gavin Hastings initiated the recovery with a penalty goal, Ieuan Evans and Rory Underwood added tries, and the captain himself scored the winner as well as converting all three. Down in the South Island, the Lions continued with a respectable win over Canterbury by 28–10 at Lancaster Park, Christchurch, but it was then that the tour stuttered as the Lions let slip an 18–13 half-time lead at Carisbrook, Dunedin. Otago pulled back to win with five tries to two.

That was the match in which Scott Hastings was injured, and the Lions also lost Wade Dooley that weekend. The English lock had to fly home because of his father's death, and though Eddie Tonks, the New Zealand Rugby Union chairman, offered Dooley an open invitation to return to the tour as and when he wished, the Home Union Tours Committee refused to sanction the bereaved forward's flight back Down Under when he decided he would like to rejoin the tour for the last two weeks. The official ruling from home was that Dooley was off the tour, he had been replaced, and consequently he could not be restored to the numbers. Rules are rules, the committee said – to which Geoff Cooke, the Lions tour manager, sharply replied by accusing Ronnie Dawson and Bob Weighill, the committee's chairman and secretary, of being 'insensitive'.

Cooke's voice was calm as he stated his views to the press corps assembled at Eden Park for the Lions' Friday practice before the Auckland match, but his anger was unconcealed. 'It's an appalling way to treat a person who has given so much to the game,' the manager suggested. Dooley had already intimated that he would retire from rugby after the tour, ending a career in which he had played 55 times for England as well as two Tests for the 1989 Lions in Australia.

Three days after the Lions' Dunedin defeat their midweek problems showed through emphatically for the first time, though the tourists cruised to a 34–16 victory over Southland at Homestead Stadium, Invercargill. The Lions took a big lead without being extended, going to 24–0 in 28 minutes with four penalty goals by Gavin Hastings, and they went on to win a messy game without taking control. It was far from ideal as the preliminary to the first Test, especially when Scott Gibbs, Rob Andrew, and Stuart Barnes had to be replaced in the course of the match. Gibbs had been shaping up well as a Test candidate, but the Welsh centre's damaged ankle ligaments prevented him from being considered for the first Test.

For that match the Lions chose a compote of nine Englishmen, four Scots, Ieuan Evans from Wales, and Nick Popplewell from Ireland, and though the overall team performance was not of the highest quality they had good reason to be frustrated by defeat. The All Blacks were surprisingly tentative despite their easy start, when Frank Bunce scored the only try of the game. After less than two minutes Fox hoisted a garryowen into the breeze. It dropped tantalisingly on to the Lions' goal-line, Bunce and Evans jumped together to gather on the bounce, and the New Zealander was judged to have grounded the ball before he was turned by the Welsh wing. Afterwards Evans was adamant that he had prevented Bunce from touching down, and compounding the Lions' annoyance, Brian Kinsey, the Australian referee, admitted that he had not seen whether the New Zealander had grounded the ball. The referee said that as his view was obscured he had relied on a nod from his compatriot, Andrew Cole, the near-side touch judge. Yet Cole was not in an ideal position to see whether a try had been scored. Bunce and Evans had their backs to the touch judge as they fell to ground.

Cooke was not so concerned by that decision as he was by the penalty against Richards that allowed Fox to kick the winning goal with two minutes left. Kinsey explained that he had penalised the Lions' number 8 for preventing the ball's release from a tackle. Yet the ball was clearly available, and Dewi Morris, the Lions' scrum-half, was picking it up as Kinsey blew his whistle for the penalty.

Despite defeat the tourists emerged with valuable credits, not least in the English breakaway trio of Clarke, Richards, and Winterbottom. Collectively, the threesome were secure in defence, often tackling beyond the gain line. Clarke merited special credit for adapting admirably to the role of blind-side flanker quite apart from his early takes at the line-out tail and occasional far-ranging support, and Winterbottom defied his pre-tour critics by outplaying Michael Jones in speed to the breakdown. The veteran of the 1983 Lions tour in New Zealand responded to McGeechan's call for him to produce a handful of top games before retirement. It was a vital facet in keeping the Lions in the hunt, especially as the once-supreme Jones was far enough off the pace to have to resort to attempting to kill the ball at the tackle. Jones cost the All Blacks two of the six Hastings penalty goals. Such tactics hampered the contest. Yet the Lions backs had it in them to have prompted victory if they

Gavin's shot. Scotland v Ireland

could have believed in their own ability in the first half. They had the platform. Martin Bayfield emerged as the Lions' dominant line-out force, and a tight five including three Scots, Burnell, Milne, and Reed, ensured the scrummage base.

After Bunce's early try the Lions had scope to respond off Bayfield and Clarke in the line-out. Rob Andrew's kick placements, however, were not precise enough, and Jeremy Guscott only once escaped to threaten, when he chipped ahead and gathered on the run. More would have come of that had not Michael Jones impeded the supporting Will Carling, though it was the occasion for Hastings to kick his third penalty goal.

It was not until Hastings had cut New Zealand to 17–15 after 52 minutes that the Lions generated more confidence in their running ability. Psychologically, too, the tourists may have been helped by hearing the Lancaster Park crowd jeering Fox for attempting a drop goal instead of expanding the All Blacks' game. Hastings, Morris, Clarke, and Winterbottom found spaces, and Rory Underwood had two long runs on the left, denied each time by John Timu. The captain's sixth penalty goal was just reward, and the Lions did not deserve to be slapped so severely by fate when Fox kicked the All Blacks winner.

All in all, after the victory over Canterbury it was an inauspicious visit to the South Island, with two Saturday defeats sandwiching an unimpressive midweek win, but the Lions' return across the Cook Strait brought a change of fortune, however temporary. The 49–25 win against Taranaki was a bright, refreshing response by the midweek team to the Test defeat, with the Lions scoring six tries to three. Vincent Cunningham, the Irish centre who replaced Scott Hastings on the tour, marked his Lions debut with two of the tries whereas Gibbs, recovered from injury, and Johnson played themselves into the Saturday team and consequently the XV for the second Test.

The Lions' New Plymouth result, though, was a false dawn. Auckland, Ranfurly Cup holders since 1985, beat the tourists 23–18 at Eden Park, and Hawke's Bay excelled themselves with a 29–17 victory at McLean Park, Napier. In each of those games the Lions led at half-time but failed to score after the interval.

Ieuan Evans, maintaining his sequence of scoring a try in each of his four non-Test games, helped the Lions to 18–11 against Auckland. Sloppy play infield, however, denied Evans two other potential chances whereas an equally notable world-class wing, John Kirwan, back in New Zealand after a season in Italian club rugby, signalled his return with a try for the Ranfurly Shield holders. Gavin Hastings had to retire from the game at half-time with a hamstring injury, Carling taking over out of position at full-back, but, ironically, it was the Lions' forwards whose game declined in the second half. Auckland profited, though only with four Fox penalty goals to turn deficit into victory.

At half-time in the Napier match the Lions were 17–5 ahead, though it was an uneasy lead as Jarrod Cunningham had missed five goals. Hawke's Bay, led from hooker by Stormin' Norman Hewitt, were not so profligate in the second half as they scored 24 points without reply.

Defeat in Napier was an unhappy prelude to the second Test at Athletic Park, especially when added to the background of the previous weeks. Since their win over the Maoris on the same ground four weeks earlier the tourists had lost all three Saturday matches, including the first Test, but Hastings – fully recovered from his Auckland injury – and his Lions were undismayed. The team was recast from the first Test, with Gibbs displacing Carling at centre in addition to the demise of the three Scottish forwards, and not only did the Lions square the series but they left the All Blacks looking as ragged as few New Zealand teams can have been in the past. It was only the British Isles' sixth win in 34 Tests in New Zealand since 1904, and the margin of 20–7 was the widest that any Lions have enjoyed. McGeechan claimed that the Lions' first-half game into the mild northerly breeze was one of the most complete team performances he had seen.

Not even a Hastings mistake swayed the Lions from their objective. The captain fumbled Fox's mortar bomb to the goal-line after 13 minutes, Eroni Clarke pounced for the try, and Fox converted. In the second quarter, kicking into the breeze, Hastings missed two penalty goals but struck a couple over, and he had another brace in the second half. By contrast, as a measure of the Lions' control, they did not allow Fox within penalty range until the first minute of the second half. He missed that and a subsequent one.

Eleven of the 15 Lions were Englishmen – after the departure of Burnell, Milne, and Reed – but it was a tale also with important characters in a Scotsman, a Welshman, an Irishman, and a Frenchman. Hastings was the inspirational key that kept the Lions locked on course after the All Blacks' try, Gibbs played like Scott Hastings at his best with thumping security in the tackle as well as the threat of suddenly puncturing the opposition, and Popplewell, marrying sound scrummaging and eager mobility, continued to enhance his growing reputation as the most complete loose-head prop to emerge from British Isles rugby for many a year. Patrick Robin also contributed. The French referee waived frustration with precise application of the tackle law and adherence to the stricter definition of ruck and maul offside. Sean Fitzpatrick, the New Zealand captain, suffered more than most on both counts.

Playing credits among the Lions were due also to Clarke, Winterbottom, Morris, and Andrew. Winterbottom's career blazed in a glorious sunset, Clarke was almost phenomenal in his work-rate and sound defence that was typified by one tackle that not only stopped Kirwan in his tracks but drove the intruding wing fearsomely backwards. Morris had his steadiest rugby of the tour, and Andrew played with control reminiscent of his game that thwarted Scotland in the 1991 World Cup semi-final at Murrayfield. Especially in the second half, the stand-off turned the All Blacks with deep diagonal kicks to the right touchline.

Nothing, however, more than the line-out provided the basis for victory quite apart from Bayfield's take for Andrew's drop goal that put the Lions ahead for the first time at 9–7 immediately before the interval. Bayfield and Johnson – who had displaced Reed – so dominated the touchline in the first half that the All Blacks were forced to regret the change that brought in Mark Cooksley to replace Ian Jones after the first Test. A hamstring injury to Cooksley – suspicious though it was – conveniently allowed Jones back into the fray at half-time, and thereafter the line-out contest was more even.

Leonard appeared to be under scrummage pressure before the interval, but he and the others locked in for two crucial scrums on the Lions' goal-line midway in the second half after two typical tackles by Ben Clarke on Kirwan. The All Blacks were held on the first of those scrums, and with the turn-over the Lions utilised the second for Andrew to relieve the siege. Almost immediately Fitzpatrick lost possession around halfway. The offering was swept up, and Guscott, with feint and swerve, sent Rory Underwood away. The wing's pace was too much for Kirwan and Timu, and his try gave the Lions the comfort of a 17–7 cushion.

New Zealand's responses to defeat were to recall Arran Pene at number 8 and introduce Lee Stensness, who, as inside centre, had looked the part of a future All Black in playing for Auckland against the Lions. Before the deciding Test, however,

Scott Hastings back home from the Lions tour, holding a ball signed by the Lions squad

the Lions had to suffer ignominy under Waikato's hands. The champions were 15 points clear after as many minutes, and they had clocked up five tries before Richard Wallace's strong run gave Carling the scope to score the Lions' only try.

After 22 minutes of the third Test the Lions were ten points up. It ought to have been the platform for victory in the match and the series. Instead, two New Zealand tries in the space of three minutes late in the first half overturned the tourists' lead, and the All Blacks went on to a handsome 30–13 win.

It was a game of 'might-have-beens' for the Lions. Three times Evans threatened on the right wing before he was snuffed out in the New Zealand 22, but the most agonising of the Lions' near-misses was when Hastings was denied on the break with Rory Underwood seemingly clear outside. A try then would have taken the Lions back into the lead at 18–17 midway in the second half. Hastings claimed afterwards that he had taken the right option when Kirwan was drifting to cover Underwood. Yet only the previous week Underwood had had the legs to beat Kirwan in scoring a Test try.

It was, however, more than the All Blacks' two first-half tries that swung the match. The manner of the New Zealand game was even more influential. They had been loose and anxious in the first quarter, but in responding to a Gibbs try the All Blacks tightened their rugby. Suddenly they became more purposeful and positive. They looked more like the 1987 World Cup champions than the 1991 All Blacks whose game had been too limited to retain the trophy.

Fox varied his attack options. He struck pressure kicks on Hastings, released flat passes to the eager Stensness, or allowed Jon Preston and the breakaways to take the ball close to source. Pene, more of a driving force than Zinzan Brook had been at number 8, was the catalyst for Jamie Joseph and Michael Jones. Joseph had an outstanding game in the line-out as well as the loose whereas he had been almost anonymous in the second Test.

As a corollary, the fire of the Lions' aggressive defence was doused, and the tourists' breakaways inevitably had a reduced impact on the match. Richards played less of the game beyond the gain line, and Clarke's rangy, ranging rugby was subdued, though the flanker still found the means for a long, loping run into the left corner after the All Blacks had stretched to 20–13.

New Zealand's response to that Clarke threat was a fearsome assault reminiscent of their first-half scoring surge. That second blitz took the All Blacks away to 27–13 with a Preston try, though Fox could have scored two as well. First, instead of diving over, the stand-off passed, allowing Underwood to intercept, and when Underwood was caught in a vain attempt to run out from the Lions 22 Fox hesitated to pick up the ball as it bounced on the goal-line.

New Zealand's scrummaging was more compact. Indeed, the Lions looked as though they had not done enough practice in that essential sphere in the week after Wellington, but it was the line-out in which the All Blacks effected the most significant turnabout after they had been outplayed by the Lions for much of the second Test. Not even the loss of Ian Jones midway in the first half upset New Zealand's touchline game. Robin Brooke and Joseph took over as the key figures in ensuring that the All Blacks could answer Bayfield's towering presence.

Stensness, oozing confidence in his first Test, made New Zealand's opening try with a deft kick through, and overall the newcomer posed problems with the variety of his game. He also drew the best out of Gibbs. The Swansea centre was as secure as anyone in the Lions' ranks quite apart from scoring his first international try after 18 unproductive games for Wales. It was a try born much in the way Underwood had scored in the second Test, with exploitation of a New Zealand fumble. Pene knocked on from a back-row ploy around halfway, Clarke swept up the loose ball, Underwood scampered into the 22, Morris and Winterbottom tried to pick holes in pockets, and when Andrew fed inside to Underwood the gap opened. Bunce blocked the pass, but Gibbs gathered and twisted over between the posts. Hastings converted, adding to his earlier penalty goal.

New Zealand swiftly responded. Joseph's line-out take released Michael Jones for Stensness to chip through for Bunce to gather and run behind the posts, and almost immediately, despite squirting scrummage ball, Fox scooped up for the breenging Va'aiga Tuigamala to intrude off the blind side and spark off an assault in which Stensness, Kirwan, Timu, and Joseph each had a go before Fitzpatrick, the All Blacks' captain, drove over for the try.

Hastings had a second penalty goal 11 minutes into the second half. It hoisted the captain past 100 points for the tour and cut the All Blacks to 17–13, but the Lions were allowed no closer. Preston's try took New Zealand 14 points clear, the scrum-half beating Hastings on the blind side of a scrum-five after a prolonged goal-line siege.

Fox converted all three tries as well as kicking three penalty goals for an international tally of 605 points – only the second player to pass 600, following his counterpart across the Tasman, Michael Lynagh. The New Zealand stand-off had 32 points in the series, six fewer than Hastings, but none of Fox's 12 goals was more important for the All Blacks or more cruel for the Lions than the one that won the first Test. It tipped the balance of the series.

**The Royal Bank
of Scotland**

McEwan's National League Results 1992–93

26 September 1992

DIVISION 1

Watsonians	13	Melrose	14
Edinburgh Academicals	18	Currie	14
Stirling County	8	Jed-Forest	9
Hawick	39	Selkirk	8
Kelso	24	Glasgow High/Kelvinside	14
Dundee HSFP	27	Heriots FP	9
Gala	11	Boroughmuir	9

DIVISION 2

Edinburgh Wanderers	25	Dunfermline	9
Kilmarnock	0	Preston Lodge FP	14
Grangemouth	25	Wigtownshire	10
Glasgow Academicals	13	West of Scotland	21
Clarkston	10	Peebles	16
Musselburgh	20	Ayr	3
Kirkcaldy	12	Stewart's/Melville FP	19

DIVISION 3

Portobello FP	23	Hillhead/Jordanhill	7
Morgan Academy FP	9	Biggar	20
Langholm	24	Royal High	13
Perthshire	30	Gordonians	0
Corstorphine	20	Dumfries	11
St Boswells	20	Howe of Fife	17
Hutchesons/Aloysians	14	Haddington	7

DIVISION 4

Leith Academicals	8	Alloa	6
Livingston	17	Cambuslang	26
East Kilbride	14	Highland	6
Lismore	23	Edinburgh University	12
Aberdeen GSFP	8	Dalziel HSFP	12
Cartha Queens Park	20	Linlithgow	14
Stewartry	19	Trinity Academicals	16

DIVISION 5

Falkirk	20	Lenzie	13
North Berwick	30	Paisley	13
Irvine	39	Madras College FP	5
Aberdeenshire	31	Moray	0
Glenrothes	9	Ardrossan Academicals	16
Clydebank	30	Penicuik	22
Waysiders	16	Hillfoots	3

DIVISION 6

Marr	5	Broughton FP	5
Cumbernauld	13	Harris Academy FC	7
Duns	35	Earlston	6
Forrester FP	20	Murrayfield	23
Dunbar	0	Berwick	34
St Andrews University	28	Drumpellier	12
Lasswade	12	Greenock Wanderers	10

DIVISION 7

Garnock	16	Stirling University	14
Strathmore	33	Carnoustie HSFP	0
Hyndland FP	8	Ross High	12
RAF Kinloss	34	Walkerburn	0
Holy Cross	16	Allan Glens	12
Montrose	18	Panmure	7
Waid Academy FP	8	Whitecraigs	18

3 October 1992

DIVISION 1

Watsonians	5	Gala	13
Heriots FP	3	Boroughmuir	12
Glasgow High/Kelvinside	41	Dundee HSFP	0
Selkirk	8	Kelso	28
Jed-Forest	15	Hawick	12
Currie	22	Stirling County	14
(played 30/1)			
Melrose	14	Edinburgh Academicals	9

DIVISION 2

Edinburgh Wanderers	11	Kirkcaldy	19
Ayr	24	Stewart's/Melville FP	35
Peebles	3	Musselburgh	17
West of Scotland	26	Clarkston	12
Wigtownshire	7	Glasgow Academicals	55
Preston Lodge FP	34	Grangemouth	99
Dunfermline	27	Kilmarnock (played 19/12)	10

DIVISION 3

Portobello FP	17	Hutchesons/Aloysians	3
Howe of Fife	8	Haddington	41
Dumfries	49	St Boswells	6

Gordonians	15	Corstorphine	3
Royal High	7	Perthshire	0
Biggar	15	Langholm	9
Hillhead/Jordanhill	11	Morgan Academy FP	20

DIVISION 4

Leith Academicals	14	Stewartry	26
Linlithgow	0	Trinity Academicals	24
Dalziel HSFP	6	Cartha Queens Park	0
Edinburgh University	7	Aberdeen GSFP	29
Highland	29	Lismore	13
Cambuslang	0	East Kilbride	11
Alloa	24	Livingston	0

DIVISION 5

Falkirk	8	Waysiders	0
Penicuik	8	Hillfoots	3
Ardrossan Academicals	25	Clydebank	5
Moray	17	Glenrothes	6
Madras College FP	3	Aberdeenshire	13
Paisley	13	Irvine	11
Lenzie	6	North Berwick	28

DIVISION 6

Marr	8	Lasswade	0
Drumpellier	13	Greenock Wanderers	27
Berwick	43	St Andrews University	6

Murrayfield	28	Dunbar	10
Earlston	10	Forrester FP	17
Harris Academy FP	20	Duns (played 21/11)	29
Broughton FP	13	Cumbernauld	12

DIVISION 7

Garnock	17	Waid Academy FP	25
Panmure	10	Whitecraigs	22
Allan Glens	34	Montrose	5
Walkerburn	3	Holy Cross	32
Ross High	13	RAF Kinloss	0
Carnoustie HSFP	12	Hyndland FP	23
Stirling University	5	Strathmore	3

10 October 1992

DIVISION 1

Boroughmuir	38	Glasgow High/Kelvinside	18
Edinburgh Academicals	16	Watsonians	12
Stirling County	13	Melrose	9
Hawick	31	Currie	11
Kelso	13	Jed-Forest	18
Dundee HSFP	12	Selkirk	18
Gala	35	Heriots FP	28

DIVISION 2

Stewart's/Melville FP	37	Peebles	0
Kilmarnock	25	Edinburgh Wanderers	13
Grangemouth	25	Dunfermline	0
Glasgow Academicals	34	Preston Lodge FP	10
Clarkston	38	Wigtownshire	6
Musselburgh	24	West of Scotland	13
Kirkcaldy	13	Ayr	6

DIVISION 3

Haddington	20	Dumfries	8
Morgan Academy FP	20	Portobello FP	13
Langholm	10	Hillhead/Jordanhill	7
Perthshire	0	Biggar	40
Corstorphine	0	Royal High	30
St Boswells	10	Gordonians	59
Hutchesons/Aloysians	16	Howe of Fife	24

DIVISION 4

Trinity Academicals	25	Dalziel HSFP	7
Livingston	12	Leith Academicals	20
East Kilbride	23	Alloa	18
Lismore	15	Cambuslang	25
Aberdeen GSFP	12	Highland	13
Cartha Queens Park	12	Edinburgh University	6
Stewartry	20	Linlithgow	5

DIVISION 5

Hillfoots	16	Ardrossan Academicals	3
North Berwick	19	Falkirk	0
Irvine	18	Lenzie	13
Aberdeenshire	42	Paisley	12
Glenrothes	18	Madras College FP	6
Clydebank	51	Moray	9
Waysiders	3	Penicuik (played 28/11)	29

DIVISION 6

Greenock Wanderers	43	Berwick	13
Cumbernauld	0	Marr	20
Duns	68	Broughton FP	5
Forrester FP	24	Harris Academy FP	15
Dunbar	8	Earlston	3
St Andrews University	37	Murrayfield	0
Lasswade	41	Drumpellier	12

DIVISION 7

Whitecraigs	13	Allan Glens	25
Strathmore	6	Garnock	15
Hyndland FP	26	Stirling University	5
RAF Kinloss	20	Carnoustie HSFP	12
Holy Cross	8	Ross High	9
Montrose	28	Walkerburn	13
Waid Academy FP	16	Panmure	10

17 October 1992

DIVISION 1

Watsonians	15	Stirling County	24
Edinburgh Academicals	33	Gala	20
Glasgow High/Kelvinside	56	Heriots FP	13
Selkirk	17	Boroughmuir	39
Jed-Forest	20	Dundee HSFP	9
Currie	33	Kelso	23
Melrose	20	Hawick	14

Rowan Shepherd of Edinburgh Accies escapes the clutches of Ian Howden of Boroughmuir to score a try

DIVISION 2

Edinburgh Wanderers	20	Grangemouth	12
Kilmarnock	17	Kirkcaldy	29
Peebles	10	Ayr	15
West of Scotland	18	Stewart's/Melville FP	23
Wigtownshire	6	Musselburgh	20
Preston Lodge FP	16	Clarkston	22
Dunfermline	18	Glasgow Academicals	26

DIVISION 4

Portobello FP	59	Langholm	0
Morgan Academy FP	3	Hutchesons/Aloysians	24
Dumfries	25	Howe of Fife	23
Gordonians	5	Haddington	41
Royal High	15	St Boswells	14
Biggar	41	Corstorphine	3
Hillhead/Jordanhill	23	Perthshire	16

DIVISION 4

Leith Academicals	19	East Kilbride	52
Livingston	3	Stewartry	16
Dalziel HSFP	16	Linlithgow	12
Edinburgh University	10	Trinity Academicals	27
Highland	3	Cartha Queens Park	10
Cambuslang	22	Aberdeen GSFP	38
Alloa	15	Lismore	10

DIVISION 5

Falkirk	10	Irvine	14
North Berwick	27	Waysiders	14
Ardrossan Academicals	41	Penicuik	0
Moray	27	Hillfoots	13
Madras College FP	13	Clydebank	16
Paisley	12	Glenrothes	14
Lenzie	24	Aberdeenshire	9

DIVISION 6

Marr	6	Duns	8
Cumbernauld	3	Lasswade	19
Berwick	50	Drumpellier (played 28/11)	0
Murrayfield	0	Greenock Wanderers	22
Earlston	19	St Andrews University	14
Harris Academy FP	27	Dunbar	3
Broughton FP	21	Forrester FP	17

DIVISION 7

Garnock	10	Hyndland FP	16
Strathmore	5	Waid Academy FP	45
Allan Glens	33	Panmure	0
Walkerburn	9	Whitecraigs	20
Ross High	23	Montrose	7
Carnoustie HSFP	12	Holy Cross	40
Stirling University	0	RAF Kinloss	24

24 October 1992

DIVISION 1

Boroughmuir	27	Jed-Forest	10
Heriots FP	33	Selkirk	20
Stirling County	3	Edinburgh Academicals	16
Hawick	11	Watsonians	14
Kelso	13	Melrose	50
Dundee HSFP	11	Currie	13
Gala	28	Glasgow High/Kelvinside	3

DIVISION 2

Stewart's/Melville FP	19	Wigtownshire	24
Ayr	8	West of Scotland	29
Grangemouth	14	Kilmarnock	20
Glasgow Academicals	28	Edinburgh Wanderers	12
Clarkston	39	Dunfermline	15
Musselburgh	23	Preston Lodge FP	14
Kirkcaldy	3	Peebles	3

DIVISION 3

Haddington	30	Royal High	3
Howe of Fife	11	Gordonians	6
Langholm	9	Morgan Academy FP	5
Perthshire	28	Portobello FP	9
Corstorphine	15	Hillhead/Jordanhill	0

| St Boswells | 12 | Biggar | 41 |
| Hutchesons/Aloysians | 24 | Dumfries | 16 |

DIVISION 4

Trinity Academicals	23	Highland	8
Linlithgow	13	Edinburgh University	10
East Kilbride	15	Livingston	6
Lismore	12	Leith Academicals	15
Aberdeen GSFP	44	Alloa	5
Cartha Queens Park	8	Cambuslang	11
Stewartry	15	Dalziel HSFP	10

DIVISION 5

Hillfoots	16	Madras College FP	21
Penicuik	18	Moray	10
Irvine	3	North Berwick	0
Aberdeenshire	15	Falkirk	11
Glenrothes	30	Lenzie	5
Clydebank	36	Paisley	12
Waysiders	11	Ardrossan Academicals	18

DIVISION 6

Greenock Wanderers	15	Earlston	17
Drumpellier	10	Murrayfield	25
Duns	64	Cumbernauld	10
(played 29/11)			
Forrester FP	16	Marr	15

Dunbar	12	Broughton FP	0
St Andrews University	6	Harris Academy FP	15
Lasswade	11	Berwick	16

DIVISION 7

Whitecraigs	19	Ross High	14
Panmure	59	Walkerburn	3
Hyndland FP	27	Strathmore	7
RAF Kinloss	35	Garnock	5
Holy Cross	43	Stirling University	3
Montrose	27	Carnoustie HSFP	15
Waid Academy FP	20	Allan Glens	0

31 October 1992

DIVISION 1

Watsonians	27	Kelso	17
Edinburgh Academicals	46	Hawick	12
Stirling County	9	Gala	14
Selkirk	24	Glasgow High/Kelvinside	22
Jed-Forest	14	Heriots FP	11
Currie	11	Boroughmuir	25
Melrose	46	Dundee HSFP	6

DIVISION 2

Edinburgh Wanderers	11	Clarkston	8
Kilmarnock	5	Glasgow Academicals	41
Grangemouth	13	Kirkcaldy	8
West of Scotland	16	Peebles	3
Wigtownshire	11	Ayr	17
Preston Lodge FP	12	Stewart's/Melville FP	6
Dunfermline	17	Musselburgh	10

DIVISION 3

Portobello	40	Corstorphine	19
Morgan Academy FP	12	Perthshire	9
Langholm	0	Hutchesons/Aloysians	29
Gordonians	30	Dumfries	14
Royal High	13	Howe of Fife	13
Biggar	12	Haddington	7
Hillhead/Jordanhill	39	St Boswells	7

DIVISION 4

Leith Academicals	17	Aberdeen GSFP	34
Livingston	32	Lismore	3
East Kilbride	11	Stewartry	16
Edinburgh University	5	Dalziel HSFP	13
Highland	25	Linlithgow	11
Cambuslang	13	Trinity Academicals	10
Alloa	5	Cartha Queens Park	14

DIVISION 5

Falkirk	18	Glenrothes	9
North Berwick	31	Aberdeenshire	16
Irvine	20	Waysiders	3
Moray	16	Ardrossan Academicals	21
Madras College FP	13	Penicuik	10
Paisley	27	Hillfoots	19
Lenzie	9	Clydebank	10

DIVISION 6

Marr	43	Dunbar	17
Cumbernauld	10	Forrester FP	6
Duns	46	Lasswade	6
Murrayfield	0	Berwick	47
Earlston	20	Drumpellier	8
Harris Academy FP	36	Greenock Wanderers	3
Broughton FP	16	St Andrews University	20

DIVISION 7

Garnock	6	Holy Cross	11
Strathmore	0	RAF Kinloss	15
Hyndland FP	19	Waid Academy FP	5
Walkerburn	6	Allan Glens	29
Ross High	38	Panmure	18
Carnoustie HSFP	8	Whitecraigs	15
Stirling University	3	Montrose	0

7 November 1992

DIVISION 1

Boroughmuir	0	Melrose	16
Heriots FP	18	Currie	23
Glasgow High/Kelvinside	23	Jed-Forest	13
Hawick	22	Stirling County	8
Kelso	26	Edinburgh Academicals	16
Dundee HSFP	15	Watsonians	29
Gala	43	Selkirk	10

DIVISION 2

Stewart's/Melville FP	42	Dunfermline	0
Ayr	19	Preston Lodge FP	12
Peebles	23	Wigtownshire	3
Glasgow Academicals	25	Grangemouth	10
Clarkston	47	Kilmarnock	7
Musselburgh	24	Edinburgh Wanderers	5
Kirkcaldy	24	West of Scotland	40

DIVISION 3

Haddington	53	Hillhead/Jordanhill	10
Howe of Fife	14	Biggar	9
Dumfries	36	Royal High	10
Perthshire	11	Langholm	3
Corstorphine	16	Morgan Academy FP	10

St Boswells	3	Portobello FP	31
Hutchesons/Aloysians	32	Gordonians	10

DIVISION 4

Trinity Academicals	44	Alloa	11
Linlithgow	10	Cambuslang	5
Dalziel HSFP	17	Highland	9
Lismore	10	East Kilbride	47
Aberdeen GSFP	57	Livingston	19
Cartha Queens Park	11	Leith Academicals	17
Stewartry	34	Edinburgh University	3

DIVISION 5

Hillfoots	28	Lenzie	23
Penicuik	20	Paisley	15
Ardrossan Academicals	35	Madras College FP	3
Aberdeenshire	6	Irvine	28
Glenrothes	7	North Berwick	15
Clydebank	15	Falkirk	16
Waysiders	43	Moray	20

DIVISION 6

Greenock Wanderers	52	Broughton FP	3
Drumpellier	7	Harris Academy FP	16
Berwick	24	Earlston	5
Forrester FP	0	Duns	61
Dunbar	13	Cumbernauld	8

| St Andrews University | 10 | Marr | 20 |
| Lasswade | 36 | Murrayfield | 10 |

DIVISION 7

Whitecraigs	14	Stirling University	0
Panmure	15	Carnoustie HSFP	24
Allan Glens	5	Ross High	0
RAF Kinloss	28	Hyndland FP	5
Holy Cross	28	Strathmore	8
Montrose	13	Garnock	5
Waid Academy FP	73	Walkerburn	0

14 November 1992

DIVISION 1

Watsonians	15	Boroughmuir	37
Edinburgh Academicals	43	Dundee HSFP	12
Stirling County	18	Kelso	19
Hawick	9	Gala (played 30/1)	9
Jed-Forest	18	Selkirk (played 30/1)	20
Currie	20	Glasgow High/Kelvinside	18
(played 27/3)			
Melrose	24	Heriots FP	15

DIVISION 2

Edinburgh Wanderers	13	Stewart's/Melville FP	24
Kilmarnock	20	Musselburgh	27
Grangemouth	20	Clarkston	24
Glasgow Academicals	27	Kirkcaldy	13
Wigtownshire	0	West of Scotland	8
Preston Lodge FP	6	Peebles	10
Dunfermline	0	Ayr	3

DIVISION 3

Portobello FP	3	Haddington	22
Morgan Academy FP	53	St Boswells	18
Langholm	20	Corstorphine (played 5/12)	10
Perthshire	9	Hutchesons/Aloysians	12
Royal High	21	Gordonians	11
Biggar	35	Dumfries	0
Hillhead/Jordanhill	6	Howe of Fife	10

DIVISION 4

Leith Academicals	18	Trinity Academicals	7
Livingston	12	Cartha Queens Park	0
East Kilbride	21	Aberdeen GSFP	13
Lismore	0	Stewartry	46
Highland	3	Edinburgh University	30
Cambuslang	12	Dalziel HSFP	17
Alloa	24	Linlithgow	9

DIVISION 5

Falkirk	8	Hillfoots	6
North Berwick	20	Clydebank	8
Irvine	13	Glenrothes	13
Aberdeenshire	24	Waysiders	8
Madras College FP	42	Moray	7
Paisley	7	Ardrossan Academicals	12
(played 21/11)			
Lenzie	18	Penicuik	7

DIVISION 6

Marr	12	Greenock Wanderers	3
Cumbernauld	29	St Andrews University	5
Duns	39	Dunbar	8
Forrester FP	18	Lasswade	10
Earlston	22	Murrayfield	12
Harris Academy FP	5	Berwick	0
Broughton FP	20	Drumpellier	17

DIVISION 7

Garnock	9	Whitecraigs (played 21/11)	13
Strathmore	3	Montrose	20
Hyndland	3	Holy Cross	10
RAF Kinloss	13	Waid Academy FP	15
Ross High	68	Walkerburn (played 21/11)	13
Carnoustie HSFP	10	Allan Glens	17
Stirling University	13	Panmure	20

9 January 1993

DIVISION 1

Boroughmuir	7	Edinburgh Academicals	10
Heriots FP	30	Watsonians	15
Glasgow High/Kelvinside	18	Melrose	33
Selkirk	9	Currie	12
Kelso	6	Hawick	20
Dundee HSFP	8	Stirling County	9
Gala	8	Jed-Forest	6

DIVISION 2

Stewart's/Melville FP	53	Kilmarnock	0
Ayr	22	Edinburgh Wanderers	16
Peebles	29	Dunfermline	8
West of Scotland	26	Preston Lodge FP	12
Clarkston	6	Glasgow Academicals	6
Musselburgh	23	Grangemouth	0
Kirkcaldy	55	Wigtownshire	17

DIVISION 3

Haddington	25	Morgan Academy FP	5
Howe of Fife	9	Portobello FP	0
Dumfries	12	Hillhead/Jordanhill	18
Gordonians	25	Biggar	29

Corstorphine	25	Perthshire	3
St Boswells	16	Langholm (played 30/1)	15
Hutchesons/Aloysians	27	Royal High (played 30/1)	19

DIVISION 4

Trinity Academicals	13	Livingston (played 30/1)	3
Linlithgow	10	Leith Academicals	34
Dalziel HSFP	6	Alloa	0
Edinburgh University	14	Cambuslang	0
Aberdeen GSFP	59	Lismore	12
Cartha Queens Park	8	East Kilbride (played 30/1)	24
Stewartry	17	Highland (played 30/11)	3

DIVISION 5

Hillfoots	8	North Berwick	6
Penicuik	10	Falkirk (played 21/11)	20
Ardrossan Academicals	26	Lenzie	15
Moray	11	Paisley	12
Glenrothes	24	Aberdeenshire (played 30/1)	9
Clydebank	14	Irvine	0
Waysiders	7	Madras College FP	8

DIVISION 6

Greenock Wanderers	42	Cumbernauld	0
Drumpellier	5	Marr	39
Berwick	20	Broughton FP	0

Murrayfield	13	Harris Academy FP	6
Dunbar	11	Forrester FP	9
St Andrews University	23	Duns	46
Lasswade	0	Earlston	22

DIVISION 7

Whitecraigs	34	Strathmore	5
Panmure	18	Garnock	0
Allan Glens	93	Stirling University	14
Walkerburn	7	Carnoustie HSFP	5
Holy Cross	15	RAF Kinloss	7
Montrose	10	Hyndland FP	11
Waid Academy FP	6	Ross High	16

23 January 1993

DIVISION 1

Watsonians (played 30/1)	21	Glasgow High/Kelvinside	15
Edinburgh Academicals	29	Heriots FP (played 27/3)	5
Stirling County	33	Boroughmuir (played 27/3)	6
Hawick	12	Dundee HSFP	3
Kelso	0	Gala	20
Currie	20	Jed-Forest	6
Melrose	35	Selkirk	5

Gordon McPherson gets two hands to the ball for West of Scotland against Edinburgh Wanderers

DIVISION 2

Edinburgh Wanderers	18	Peebles (played 30/1)	17
Kilmarnock	7	Ayr (played 30/1)	9
Grangemouth (played 30/1)	18	Stewart's/Melville FP	23
Glasgow Academicals	18	Musselburgh (played 30/1)	35
Clarkston	25	Kirkcaldy (played 30/1)	0
Preston Lodge FP	10	Wigtownshire	10
Dunfermline (played 30/1)	16	West of Scotland	38

DIVISION 3

Portobello FP	6	Dumfries	18
Morgan Academy FP	13	Howe of Fife (played 30/1)	30
Langholm	13	Haddington	8
Perthshire	48	St Boswells (played 30/1)	7
Corstorphine	13	Hutchesons/Aloysians	31
(played 20/3)			
Biggar	7	Royal High	6
(ab. after 40 min.)			
Biggar	29	Royal High (played 30/3)	6
Hillhead/Jordanhill	24	Gordonians	0

DIVISION 4

Leith Academicals	14	Dalziel HSFP	16
Livingston	12	Linlithgow	10
(ab. after 70 min.)			
Livingston	14	Linlithgow (played 20/3)	13
East Kilbride	28	Trinity Academicals	5
(played 20/3)			
Lismore	10	Cartha Queens Park	16
(played 27/3)			
Aberdeen GSFP	8	Stewartry	10
Cambuslang		Highland (not played)	
Alloa	10	Edinburgh University	26
(played 30/1)			

DIVISION 5

Falkirk		Ardrossan Academicals	
(not played)			
North Berwick	14	Penicuik	7
Irvine	6	Hillfoots	10
Aberdeenshire	15	Clydebank	8
Glenrothes	20	Waysiders	7
(ab. after 75 min.)			
Glenrothes	5	Waysiders (played 20/3)	5
Paisley	13	Madras College FP	10
(played 30/1)			
Lenzie	15	Moray (played 30/1)	3

DIVISION 6

Marr	0	Berwick	8
Cumbernauld	20	Drumpellier (played 30/1)	0
Duns	29	Greenock Wanderers	5
Forrester FP	9	St Andrews University	8
Dunbar	13	Lasswade	9
Harris Academy FP	10	Earlston	6
(ab. after 70 min.)			
Harris Academy FP	23	Earlston (played 30/1)	22
Broughton FP	0	Murrayfield (played 30/1)	6

DIVISION 7

Garnock	3	Allan Glens	14
Strathmore	0	Panmure	8
Hyndland FP	0	Whitecraigs	3

RAF Kinloss	5	Montrose	10
(ab. after 50 min.)			
RAF Kinloss	12	Montrose (played 30/1)	14
Holy Cross	38	Waid Academy FP	0
(played 30/1)			
Carnoustie HSFP	15	Ross High (played 30/1)	37
Stirling University	5	Walkerburn	7

13 February 1993

DIVISION 1

Boroughmuir		Hawick (not played)	
Heriots FP	24	Stirling County	7
Glasgow High/Kelvinside	13	Edinburgh Academicals	22
Selkirk	16	Watsonians	19
Jed-Forest	16	Melrose	19
Dundee HSFP	23	Kelso	16
Gala	47	Currie	13

DIVISION 2

Stewart's/Melville FP	32	Glasgow Academicals	18
Ayr	22	Grangemouth	12
Peebles	9	Kilmarnock	0
West of Scotland	35	Edinburgh Wanderers	12
Wigtownshire	13	Dumfermline	13
Musselburgh	21	Clarkston	8
Kirkcaldy	17	Preston Lodge FP	31

DIVISION 3

Haddington	21	Perthshire	0
Howe of Fife	10	Langholm	11
Dumfries	8	Morgan Academy FP	13
Gordonians	27	Portobello FP	16
Royal High	9	Hillhead/Jordanhill	16
St Boswells	6	Corstorphine	30
Hutchesons/Aloysians	14	Biggar	7

DIVISION 4

Trinity Academicals	47	Lismore	13
Linlithgow	5	East Kilbride	16
Dalziel HSFP	12	Livingston	14
Edinburgh University	38	Leith Academicals	17
Highland	11	Alloa	3
Cartha Queens Park	8	Aberdeen GSFP	23
Stewartry	36	Cambuslang	0

DIVISION 5

Hillfoots	20	Aberdeenshire	0
Penicuik	15	Irvine	10
Ardrossan Academicals	18	North Berwick	6
Moray	5	Falkirk	34
Madras College FP	13	Lenzie	8
Clydebank	20	Glenrothes	14
Waysiders	18	Paisley	6

DIVISION 6

Greenock Wanderers	10	Forrester FP	31
Drumpellier	3	Duns	70
Berwick	30	Cumbernauld	3
Murrayfield	24	Marr	12
Earlston	28	Broughton FP	13
St Andrews University	24	Dunbar	0
Lasswade	12	Harris Academy FP	5

DIVISION 7

Whitecraigs	13	RAF Kinloss	24
Panmure	10	Hyndland FP	10
Allan Glens	72	Strathmore	0
Walkerburn	3	Garnock	13
Ross High	14	Stirling University	8
Montrose	20	Holy Cross	20
Waid Academy FP	19	Carnoustie HSFP	3

27 February 1993

DIVISION 1

Watsonians	5	Jed-Forest	50
Edinburgh Academicals	6	Selkirk	6
Stirling County	23	Glasgow High/Kelvinside	11
Hawick	15	Heriots FP	20

Kelso	18	Boroughmuir	12
Dundee HSFP	16	Gala	13
Melrose	16	Currie	7

DIVISION 2

Edinburgh Wanderers	9	Wigtownshire	15
Kilmarnock	3	West of Scotland	55
Grangemouth	25	Peebles	0
Glasgow Academicals	20	Ayr	12
Clarkston	3	Stewart's/Melville FP	24
Musselburgh	25	Kirkcaldy	0
Dunfermline	18	Preston Lodge FP	18

DIVISION 3

Portobello FP	20	Royal High	6
Morgan Academy FP	0	Gordonians (played 20/3)	29
Langholm	19	Dumfries	22
Perthshire	15	Howe of Fife	8
Corstorphine	10	Haddington	12
St Boswells	3	Hutchesons/Aloysians	26
Hillhead/Jordanhill	18	Biggar	14

DIVISION 4

Leith Academicals	19	Highland	15
Livingston	0	Edinburgh University	3
East Kilbride	17	Dalziel HSFP	9
Lismore	8	Linlithgow	11

Aberdeen GSFP (not played)		Trinity Academicals	
Cartha Queens Park	11	Stewartry	15
Alloa	52	Cambuslang (played 20/3)	0

DIVISION 5

Falkirk	18	Madras College FP	0
North Berwick	58	Moray	10
Irvine	0	Ardrossan Academicals	10
Aberdeenshire		Penicuik (not played)	
Glenrothes	17	Hillfoots	12
Clydebank	19	Waysiders	9
Lenzie	19	Paisley	12

DIVISION 6

Marr	57	Earlston	3
Cumbernauld	18	Murrayfield	0
Duns	10	Berwick	9
Forrester FP	38	Drumpellier	5
Dunbar	19	Greenock Wanderers	15
St Andrews University	23	Lasswade	7
Broughton FP	18	Harris Academy FP	22

DIVISION 7

Garnock	3	Ross High	21
Strathmore	0	Walkerburn	18
Hyndland FP	5	Allan Glens	34

RAF Kinloss		Panmure (not played)	
Holy Cross	32	Whitecraigs	6
Montrose	3	Waid Academy FP	11
(played 20/3)			
Stirling University	5	Carnoustie HSFP	0

13 March 1993

DIVISION 1

Boroughmuir		Dundee HSFP (not played)	
Heriots FP	86	Kelso	8
Glasgow High/Kelvinside	39	Hawick	0
Selkirk	33	Stirling County	10
Jed-Forest	11	Edinburgh Academicals	10
Currie	19	Watsonians	6
Gala	14	Melrose	30

DIVISION 2

Stewart's/Melville FP	17	Musselburgh	14
Ayr	5	Clarkston	25
Peebles	27	Glasgow Academicals	20
West of Scotland	52	Grangemouth	6
Wigtownshire	38	Kilmarnock	6
Preston Lodge FP	15	Edinburgh Wanderers	11
Kirkcaldy	44	Dunfermline	0

DIVISION 3

Haddington	57	St Boswells	3
Howe of Fife	13	Corstorphine	13
Dumfries	23	Perthshire	17
Gordonians	5	Langholm	11
Royal High	19	Morgan Academy FP	6
Biggar	15	Portobello FP	6
Hutchesons/Aloysians	5	Hillhead/Jordanhill	20

DIVISION 4

Trinity Academicals	17	Cartha Queens Park	14
Linlithgow	19	Aberdeen GSFP	6
Dalziel HSFP	41	Lismore	12
Edinburgh University	10	East Kilbride	30
Highland	20	Livingston	10
Cambuslang	37	Leith Academicals	6
Stewartry	25	Alloa	12

DIVISION 5

Hillfoots	10	Clydebank	7
Penicuik	9	Glenrothes	16
Ardrossan Academicals	30	Aberdeenshire	9
Moray	3	Irvine	52
Madras College FP	15	North Berwick	24
Paisley	20	Falkirk	13
Waysiders	14	Lenzie	14

DIVISION 6

Greenock Wanderers	20	St Andrews University	12
Drumpellier	24	Dunbar	12
Berwick	18	Forrester FP	13
Murrayfield	10	Duns	69
Earlston	17	Cumbernauld	8
(ab. after 70 min.)			
Harris Academy FP	10	Marr	8
Lasswade	7	Broughton FP	0

DIVISION 7

Whitecraigs	24	Montrose	13
Panmure	8	Holy Cross	8
Allan Glens	52	RAF Kinloss	0
Walkerburn	36	Hyndland FP	7
Ross High	127	Strathmore	3
Carnoustie HSFP	9	Garnock	16
Waid Academy FP	17	Stirling University	34

**The Royal Bank
of Scotland**

McEwan's National League Tables 1992–93

DIVISION 1	P	W	D	L	F	A	Pts
Melrose	13	12	0	1	326	134	24
Edinburgh Academicals	13	9	1	3	265	156	19
Gala	13	9	1	3	275	171	19
Currie	13	8	0	5	218	242	16
Jed-Forest	13	7	0	6	206	185	14
Boroughmuir	11	6	0	5	206	162	12
Hawick	12	5	1	6	197	199	11
Heriot's FP	13	5	0	8	295	285	10
Stirling County	13	5	0	8	179	208	10
Watsonians	13	5	0	8	195	277	10
Kelso	13	5	0	8	211	345	10
Selkirk	13	4	1	8	194	316	9
Glasgow High/Kelvinside	13	4	0	9	291	255	8
Dundee HSFP	12	3	0	9	142	269	6

DIVISION 2	P	W	D	L	F	A	Pts
West of Scotland	13	11	0	2	377	156	22
Stewart's/Melville FP	13	11	0	2	364	156	22
Musselburgh	13	11	0	2	283	124	22
Glasgow Academicals	13	8	1	4	331	208	17
Clarkston	13	7	1	5	267	173	15
Ayr	13	7	0	6	165	210	14
Peebles	13	6	1	6	160	178	13
Preston Lodge FP	13	5	2	6	204	205	12
Kirkcaldy	13	5	1	7	233	234	11
Grangemouth	13	4	0	9	189	261	8
Edinburgh Wanderers	13	4	0	9	176	253	8
Wigtownshire	13	3	2	8	160	294	8
Dunfermline	13	2	2	9	141	322	6
Kilmarnock	13	2	0	11	120	378	4

John Amos escapes with the ball for the South against Edinburgh

DIVISION 3	P	W	D	L	F	A	Pts
Haddington	13	10	0	3	348	94	20
Biggar	13	10	0	3	307	123	20
Hutchesons/Aloysians	13	10	0	3	257	146	20
Hillhead/Jordanhill	13	7	0	6	199	194	14
Howe of Fife	13	6	2	5	190	188	14
Langholm	13	7	0	6	144	190	14
Portobello FP	13	6	0	7	221	177	12
Dumfries	13	6	0	7	242	241	12
Royal High	13	5	1	7	171	226	11
Corstorphine	13	5	1	7	173	232	11
Perthshire	10	5	0	5	186	186	10
Gordonians	13	5	0	8	220	242	10
Morgan Academy FP	13	5	0	8	169	231	10
St Boswells	13	2	0	11	125	480	4

DIVISION 4	P	W	D	L	F	A	Pts
Stewartry	13	13	0	0	295	96	28
East Kilbride	13	12	0	1	309	125	24
Dalziel High School FP	13	9	0	4	192	143	18
Trinity Academicals	12	8	0	4	258	144	16
Aberdeen GS FP	12	7	0	6	331	165	14
Leith Academicals	13	7	0	6	218	276	14
Cartha Queen's Park	13	5	0	8	132	163	10
Highland	12	5	0	7	145	179	11
Edinburgh University	13	5	0	8	174	211	10
Cambuslang	12	5	0	7	151	234	10
Alloa	13	4	0	9	185	220	8
Livingston	13	4	0	9	142	222	8
Linlithgow	13	4	0	9	132	222	8
Lismore	13	1	0	12	141	395	2

DIVISION 5	P	W	D	L	F	A	Pts
Adrossan Academicals	12	11	0	1	255	97	22
North Berwick	13	10	0	3	277	125	20
Clydebank	13	8	0	5	240	174	18
Falkirk	12	8	0	4	176	128	15
Irvine	13	7	1	5	214	115	15
Glenrothes	13	6	2	5	182	158	14
Hillfoots	13	6	0	7	164	169	12
Aberdeenshire	12	6	0	6	189	199	12
Penicuik	12	5	0	7	155	193	10
Madras College FP	13	5	0	8	152	224	10
Paisley	13	5	0	8	174	255	10
Lenzie	13	4	1	8	182	218	9
Waysiders	13	3	2	8	151	200	8
Moray	13	2	0	11	138	396	4

DIVISION 6	P	W	D	L	F	A	Pts
Duns	13	13	0	0	585	111	26
Berwick	13	10	0	3	312	96	20
Marr	13	8	0	5	245	107	16
Harris Academy FP	13	8	0	5	207	158	16
Forrester FP	13	7	0	6	218	217	14
Greenock Wanderers	13	6	0	7	287	197	12
Lasswade	13	6	0	7	170	186	12
Earlston	12	6	0	6	177	237	12
Dunbar	13	6	0	7	126	263	12
Murrayfield	13	6	0	7	151	309	12
St Andrews University	13	5	0	8	216	236	10
Cumbernauld	12	5	0	7	126	219	10
Broughton FP	13	3	0	10	112	266	8
Drumpellier	13	1	0	12	116	406	2

DIVISION 7	P	W	D	L	F	A	Pts
Allan Glen's	13	11	0	2	420	92	22
Ross High	13	11	0	2	392	113	22
Holy Cross	13	10	2	1	301	97	22
Whitecraigs	13	10	0	3	214	157	20
Waid Academy FP	13	8	0	6	260	176	16
RAF Kinloss	12	7	0	5	212	144	14
Montrose & District	13	6	1	6	170	181	13
Hyndland FP	13	6	1	6	160	182	13
Panmure	12	4	2	6	183	185	10
Garnock	13	4	0	9	115	198	8
Stirling University	13	4	0	9	109	277	5
Walkerburn	13	4	0	9	118	373	8
Carnoustie High School FP	13	1	0	12	125	274	2
Strathmore	13	1	0	12	73	414	2

Promoted from
District Leagues West: Annan, East, Dalkeith, North &
Midlands, Aberdeen University

**The Royal Bank
of Scotland**

McEwan's Inter-District Championship

	P	W	D	L	F	A	Pts
South	4	3	0	1	60	33	6
Edinburgh	4	2	1	1	93	69	5
North and Midlands	4	2	0	2	60	101	4
Glasgow	4	1	1	2	44	59	3
Scottish Exiles	4	1	0	3	57	52	2

North and Midlands	3	South	26	(Mayfield)
Edinburgh	13	Glasgow	13	(Goldenacre)
Glasgow	9	South	7	(Hughenden)
North and Midlands	18	Edinburgh	45	(Countesswells)
Scottish Exiles	17	Glasgow	7	(Richmond)
South	8	Scottish Exiles	6	(Mansfield Park)
Glasgow	15	North and Midlands	22	(Burnbrae)
Edinburgh	20	Scottish Exiles	19	(Meggetland)
South	19	Edinburgh	15	(The Greenyards)
Scottish Exiles	15	North and Midlands	17	(Northampton)

The 1993 Five Nations Championship

	P	W	D	L	F	A	Pts
France	4	3	0	1	73	35	6
Scotland	4	2	0	2	50	40	4
England	4	2	0	2	54	54	4
Ireland	4	2	0	2	45	53	4
Wales	4	1	0	3	34	74	2

Scotland	15	Ireland	3	(Murrayfield)*
England	16	France	15	(Twickenham)
France	11	Scotland	3	(Parc des Princes)
Wales	10	England	9	(Cardiff Arms Park)
Scotland	20	Wales	0	(Murrayfield)*
Ireland	6	France	21	(Lansdowne Road)
England	26	Scotland	12	(Twickenham)
Wales	14	Ireland	19	(Cardiff Arms Park)
France	26	Wales	10	(Parc des Princes)
Ireland	17	England	3	(Lansdowne Road)

*Royal Bank of Scotland International